I Am God's Dream

MICHAEL K. ASHER

ISBN 979-8-88943-878-6 (paperback)
ISBN 979-8-88943-879-3 (digital)

Christian Faith Publishing
832 Park Avenue
Meadville, PA 16335
www.christianfaithpublishing.com

Printed in the United States of America

CONTENTS

Chapter 1: Welcome to My World 1

Chapter 2: Wonder Years, Really? 6

Chapter 3: My Brother's Shadow 19

Chapter 4: I Know My Stuff 30

Chapter 5: The Working Years 41

Chapter 6: Listening and Experiencing the Hand of God 54

Chapter 7: How to Win with Jesus 62

Hello and welcome to this journey as I take you from where I came from to where I am now. This is a story about faith being used and what one experiences as one grows up and goes through life from a Christian perspective. This starts out in a small town in Connecticut where a family of six were making it happen. This may sound ordinary, but as you take on this journey, you'll see the extraordinary hand of God working in the life of one who did not want to get it wrong.

CHAPTER 1

Welcome to My World

Hello and welcome to my world. It's not just a plain, ordinary world. There is so much that has happened behind the scenes. There is no telling the direction and protection I was receiving since I was born. So this is where it all began. My world was made in Connecticut. We had two houses in the same town over the course of my childhood. One was in the early years; when I was born at a very young age I might add. We lived on the main road but in a small house with a barn and a big field. It was big enough for me as a two-year-old to get scared. I can remember so many memories even in my late forties when you'd see me now on IG and in some power bodybuilding post, you'd say I am in my early thirties. Thank God and my parents for good genetics there. However, there is something more really behind my birth and the decisions I made. Some were made for me in miracles that saved my life. I want to let you know this isn't a memoir to boast about but to help you see that you are more important than you'll ever know.

Just to take you down the small country road of memory lane. I can tell you that our first house had a big field with tall grass, timothy they call it. I was no bigger than that when I can remember my brother running alongside my father as he was on a green tractor he borrowed from a neighbor to do some haying. I was wearing red shorts and a white T-shirt and still in diapers, and boy when he turned around, I ran as fast as I could back up to the house as I thought I was going to get run over—that and memories of our black cat with a white spot on its nose who bit my finger and it bled. Yes, we were country folks. Our lives changed when my father had a job opportunity that took us to Alabama for a few years. Quite a few things happened down in Alabama but not worth mentioning here as most of it affected my parents, although I do remember riding my brother's bike that was too big for me and wiping out in the sand at the end of the street only to wake up in his arms as he carried me home. Moving on.

We did move back in 1980 and settled on Golden Brook Rd. This house was the first house on the block that had an in-ground pool. It was something! It was next to the road, but it had a fence that was seven feet tall all the way around. We used to have friends from church come and swim in the summertime. We must have had every single family over. Because I guess it was the thing. One of the first two houses to have an in-ground pool. Our house was a three-bedroom cape made in the '40s or '50s good solid construction of white pine and plaster walls. Trust me, my head knows those walls are solid.

Back then it was. What seemed to be a big house when I was small turned to be a small house when I got older. This was my childhood home. I experienced everything that I'm about to tell you while living in this house. Let's get started, and let me tell you a little bit about what happened to me as a child, a teen, and as an adult.

God is at work in our lives, and He wants us all to come to Him and be His children. 2 Peter 3:9 states,

> The Lord is not slack concerning His promise as some men count slackness but as longsuffering to us word not willing that *any* should perish but that all should come to repentance. (italics mine)

This one verse alone will let you know just how special you are, and I'm going to show you how many times my life has been saved, the warning signs that I could have, should have listened to, and some that just happened by *accident*. One involves a car, another

80-mph pop fly, and other situations where the sixth sense, the Holy Spirit, helped guide my decisions.

I was the youngest of four. There was the oldest brother, then a sister, and then another older brother. The oldest brother's name was John. John was a unique individual as we all were, but among us, he stood out as the black sheep in the family. I can remember waking up in the morning to hear him screaming down the stairs to my mother that he wasn't going to school or something else. He definitely stressed my mother out. Just to set the time frame, this all happened in the early '80s. I am a child of the '80s.

John was under the influence of music and bad friends. He loved music, and sound influences our bodies because we were made to worship, to sing, and to praise God. He used to listen to the Doors, Kiss, and all that hair band stuff. Some of the music that he listened to probably wasn't the greatest influence nor were the friends that he was hanging out with of any better influence either. John would not be the one who would sit in the front row at church or be always in church. In fact, there were times when he was so bad that he would interrupt a church service. How embarrassing. I would shrink in my seat as everyone would look over at the attention he was drawing. Most times he sat in the back row and caused all these issues if he was there at all. I can recall the stories of us being dropped off for Sunday school, and I think he would go down to the local store and buy something or whatever not attend his class and then come back when it was time to go home. He had a real problem with authority.

John went to school as most students did, but because of his behavior and his issues with authority, he was suspended from two high school systems and was kicked out. He never finished high school till much later in life. Life did teach him, and he did learn but he was a slow learner, was thickheaded, and was full of pride, but life beat him, and God saved him again. It's not that he wasn't saved and that he didn't know God; it's just that he wasn't allowing God to lead and direct him (like a prodigal son). Some battle was taking place between John and Satan, and we didn't know why. We're not sure whether it was Satan trying to get ahold of him and destroy him or through him destroy us. You know how this goes like with the

Bible and its historical view of what happened with all the attempts made to distort the line of David in which our savior Jesus was born. We can find this as far back as Genesis 6, and further even with the temptation of Eve in the garden. In Genesis 6, there were giants that were the byproduct of fallen angels and the women of Earth. As you read, maybe you and I will find out together what was the plan of God versus the plan of Satan for our family.

John was six feet two inches, in his prime. He was the best bad-boy older brother one could ever have. He liked tinkering with tools and dirt bikes, most notably Honda dirt bikes. So he coined himself the one wheel rider. He was very good at what he did. He could ride, and he could take a bike apart, have it all in pieces, and have it rebuilt in three days. He had a head for this mechanical part. He also had a great deal of balance. He would get on a dirt bike, start riding, and pull a wheelie from our house to the end of the street, and then he would turn around and ride it back up on one wheel. He was definitely one talented individual.

But something had a hold on him. Something was really confusing him, distracting him, and pulling him aside. When I mean pulling him aside, I mean taking him away from obeying Mom and Dad and doing the right thing, from his behavior in class and his interactions with authority. He didn't do anything bad like mean or evil things. He just wouldn't do what he was told, he wouldn't stay on the right path. John had so many cases involving breaking the law.

I remember hearing a knock at the door one night and seeing the top of a state trooper's hat as we came down the stairs from our bedroom. We were always taught to respect law enforcement so it was an anxious time for all. Mom and Dad talked with the officer in the doorway and found out that John was wanted for something and he was tracking him down.

John had run away a few times. I think all in all, he was kicked out of the house four times. Each time, he was allowed back only if he would change. One time, he took Dad's old pickup truck and drove all the way across the USA to Washington state. It was incredible that he had the ability and courage to do that on his own. I marveled at that. There also came a time when I had the option to drive across the country a little bit for Jamie, a girl whom I thought I would marry. However I did not have the courage, and love was not as compelling as I thought it was.

John had some bad friends. He seemed to pick up the wrong crowd. I remember hearing stories of him about his excursion with his friends on the weekend or weeknights in the cars that they would drive. The cars that these guys were driving back in the day were awesome. They were muscle cars. They used to work on them at the school.

He went to a trade school first before he was kicked out. I can't remember why he was kicked out other than the fact that he just had a problem with authority and caused more distractions which probably did not allow the students to learn.

I just want to let you know that many years later, he was still around and in decent shape. He would now witness the people on the CB radio. John is now a voice of reason helping people who came from the same walk of life or with similar experiences.

CHAPTER 2

Wonder Years, Really?

While we were not sure what that fighting constantly was all about, one thing we did know was not to make the same mistakes my older brother made. So with that in mind, the last three kids did okay. We were close together in age and did a lot of things together. I think this was one good thing about siblings.

I was in grade school then. Everything was good up until about fifth grade. In the fifth grade, this was when identities, affiliations, and profiles started to take shape of who people were going to be going forward. We used to joke around on the playground at school about being in a gang. I can still remember our motto, "Mess with the best, die like the rest." It was at this time that all the childish things that we did in grades 1 through 4 were put behind us. Now was the time to see how tough we were and who we would have for friends.

In my generation, kids were just mean. They would create their own cliques and decide who was going to be in their crew and who wasn't. They would also rough people up on the playground or in the hallways or in the back of classrooms or worse yet on the bus. I had many bullies when I was growing up, despite being very tall and wearing glasses. And it wasn't the physical bully—although there was that—it was the mental berating and making fun because of my belief or conversation. It was then that I would suffer because of my belief in God for my naive understanding of the world around me that was secular. Oh, if only the walls could talk.

Enter Dan Robertson. Here we have a boy who seemed to be a bit confused in life and full of hate and envy. Looking at him, it seemed as if he was bitter at such a young age. He would always have a snippy response for anything you say or anything that you say he would twist and turn around. The teachers would even be challenged only for a bit, and then he'd get detention. In addition, he would twist and turn around on you. There were a lot of people who were also like him. I remember Scott Reynolds, who would earn your trust and sound sincere but then when he'd get far away enough from you, he would turn on you and embarrass you or attempt to embarrass you, like on the bus ride home. It seemed that lying and betrayal were the only things these kids knew. What were their home lives look like? What were their parents like? The only thing I could think of was that these kids must have felt dissension, mistrust, and loneliness. In my home, there was love and care, but because of the issues some of us had—ahem, the eldest—not all of us got the time we could have or should have received.

In the fifth grade, I broke my wrist when a bully pushed me down backward on the recess field or soccer field behind the portables. Back then, we called the quickly-built-and-not-planned buildings portables. It must have been a birth boom then in the '80s. Now back to the pain. I got up and couldn't move my fingers, and I turned to him and asked, "Why did you do that?" He felt bad and tried to pawn off his Sega or Nintendo to me. I believed he was sorry, but I had no idea what got into him.

We drove to the hospital, and there, a doctor fixed my wrist. I had to be tied down in anticipation of my response and what he was going to do next. They didn't really tie me. I self-hooked my good arm around the bar to not punch anyone. I think my mother held my legs, or the nurse did. Oh, the sound of my bone popping back into place hurt; tears flowed. How awful that a kid could cause such pain. My mother must have been really hurt seeing how someone can do this to her own son. I never did and continued to not harm people. This is what trying to show some male bravado did for most kids whose father was a real gearhead or tough enough candidate did for them. Posturing to make up for the lack of knowing the direction their life should be going as their parents is the price these children paid. Please, if you have kids, spend time with them.

One day after school, I was getting on the bus to go home. This must have been when I was in sixth grade because my brother was still in school with me and riding the bus. This was my closest brother in age; his name was David. There was a guy named Dan. Well, as Dan and I got on the bus, I was ahead of Dan and was walking down to the back of the bus to get a seat of my choice. No sooner had I found a seat to get into. That was when Dan pushed me into the seat with all his might. I was ticked off. I did not like to be treated like that. I was angry, and I started to make a move toward him. As I started to go over and raise my fist as if I was going to punch him, he punched me first, and my glasses went flying. That's right. I was a kid with glasses who knew Jesus and was told to turn the other cheek. Well, let me tell you, I did turn my cheek, my whole head turned, and my glasses flew right off.

My brother was right behind me and was getting on the bus with his friend. He saw what was going on, pushed me down into the seat gently, and then went down and held back Dan. Dan tried to take a swing at him, but he was no match; he got put in his place and then started to pout and whine that I threw the first punch. It was a bit rewarding seeing my brother David put him down, including his physical attempt at hitting him. This is just one example of some of the physical battles I had to deal with. So what was I supposed to do? Turn the other cheek and be forgiving? You know what happens when you give them an inch.

This exchange went back and forth for several years, or what felt like several years. It was most likely two more 'cause eighth grade was just around the corner. Every day I dreaded seeing these guys in school. Speaking of which, some girls were not so nice either when they were nearby. They didn't do anything physical, but they liked the bad boys. I think it was during seventh grade, and Mr. Roy was our homeroom teacher, and he allowed us to arm wrestle. He was a marine in his day and had a thing for social studies and journalism and what events were going on around the world. He was a very nice teacher. He used to have a nickname for himself, Dan Rather Roy. Dan Rather was a real evening news anchor for CBS News for many years. Like I said he liked watching the news and the events during the '80s. They were most definitely very exciting times.

Just like that, Dan and I started to arm wrestle. I beat him. I beat Dan Robertson. I thought to myself, *Wow, what is this?* like I did something extra special around the farm. How could I have beaten a bully? That was about all the respect I got from Dan. I can remember him saying "You're no slouch." Again, these were just small shorts of many of the events that would happen. It wasn't all the time that I was in a fight as I could count them on my hand. Most of the fights never took place. It was just showdowns with walk-offs. What did take place was the exchange of feelings and dislike for each other.

There was something odd about Dan as you would always see him get in trouble. He was always going to the office. His dress was okay, but he could not manage to comb his hair a little better or tuck in his shirt or even carry himself well to show respect for the people around him. He didn't do any of that often. Some days looked promising like you'd have hope for him to change. Seventh grade came and went, and then in eighth grade, it was entirely a different story. Another grade, another bully.

Harry Moore was an interesting individual. All through the years, from fifth through eighth grade, he was trying to find himself, whereas Dan was trying to lose himself. Harry spent most of his time being cool and had hair like Fonzie's in *Happy Days*. If that's too far back for all of you, just picture in place a slicked-back black hair parted down the middle. He was trying to keep up with music bands, BMX bikes, and dirt bikes. I'm not too sure what his home life was like, but it seemed as if his parents didn't have time for him either.

The era that I grew up in was the time of the technical evolution of video games. I went from the typewriter to the computer. We went from the Atari system to the Commodore 64, Nintendo, and Sega consoles. My favorite game to play on the Atari was River Raid or Pitfall Harry. Another cool game was Chopper Command. I had always wanted to be a pilot, but because of my vision and my dental issue, that wasn't in the cards. Notably, the movie that propelled this dream was *Top Gun*. Arguably, this must have been some of the tools the parents used to babysit the kids; give them what they want so they could be left alone.

Harry was one of those guys who had something to prove besides his identity. He had to prove that he was one tough customer. One day, while sitting down at the earth sciences table in the eighth-grade class of Mrs. Hall, Harry decided to take out a tac and try and swipe across my eyes on my face. Sitting next to him was Cherry Mumford. She was a very pretty girl, who would be a homecoming queen in the future at a large school in Connecticut. Who thought it was cool to be with tough guys? Well, fortunately, nothing happened to my face, but I wasn't happy. I did not back down. I told him right then and there, "Are you crazy? You can hurt someone." Well, he didn't like that. Nothing happened memorable after that. You could see though that he was looking to prove and identify who he was among his fellow students, just running his mouth and being bad during class time.

Harry was also known for his lewd behavior, crassness, and general disrespect for authority and people who would cross his path. He had a chip on his shoulder, but I don't think it was bitter. Harry was really concerned with his appearance. He looked very polished and very cool and took pride in his appearance, which is a good thing, but I was just curious why he had such ill will for someone like me. So Harry was just looking to have a good time. He was the most carnal person you would ever meet, and that was what I know from what I was able to see. Who knew what he did in private?

So here we were again at another decision point. One part of me wanted to tear this guy's head off. Another part of me wanted to stand my ground. There was never a part of me that wanted to turn away and cry. That just wasn't me. I went home from all these little incursions that I had with different people and talked to my parents about it and ask them for advice. But you know what they'd say?" "Don't get near him," "Don't hang out with them," Don't give him an inch," and "Harry starts it. You can finish it." No, they didn't say that we weren't supposed to finish the fight, but inside my mind, I always just wanted to pound them and walk away and be the hero afterward. All those movies and TV shows about the underdog we watched were just coping ways for me to say, "One day, someone is going to take a stand. One day someone is going to say, 'Enough.'"

What did I do to deserve this type of behavior? I mean really, I was just a kid, and I loved sports, minded my own business, and was very naive during the wonder years. We did have our Bible club meetings that happened on Wednesdays.

In my era, 1984, it was the first year that the Word of Life Bible Institute made a program for young kids called Olympians. We were the first kids to ever experience this program. Let me tell, you this was one of the best programs I have ever been in as a person. Going to church twice a week helped give me an edge in life like no other. Now I know this may sound strange, but I was ahead of my time because of this.

The insights that I got from studying the word of God, the Bible verses I memorized, and the stories we heard and understood, all these things, helped me develop a sixth sense. I reached a level like a sight beyond sight miraculously. Not that I was a prophet because all the prophets are done, and the Bible is complete. However, that little voice inside my head was amplified. In some cases, I could see people's faces based on their voices, and when I met them, it matched. Looking at someone and talking for a few minutes, I was able to surmise their life events. I really don't know what this advantage was at the time, but now I know it was so I could be a better witness not betting on horses or outcomes of sporting events.

Maybe this is what you would call a detective skill. A skill that law enforcement and detectives use is that hunch or gut instinct. It's like when you see someone, you read them, and you know that person even though you don't know them at all. All through my teenage years, this training, this Bible memorization, this reading the chapters, and understanding life and what's happening and what's going on around us were easier to digest and process.

No, this is not a monk thing but voluntary and passionate love and learning about the Bible and world events. There was a time in my teenage years when I thought this was it. In 1991 during the Iraq war, I thought the end of days was coming. It became so great in me that I never thought I'd get this far. How did I get this far? It's really surreal at times when you do a double take and realize you're a father, husband, son, and brother all at once. I didn't even go to college right away as I thought Christ would return. Remember, folks, do not be so heavenly minded that you are no earthly good. You must work and perform as if you are going to retire but also take time to live in the moment.

Much of my life revolved around close family gatherings because we had a decent-sized family. Our family stayed together, and we played together. I had a typical childhood. I had a banana-seat bike, the Apache. If you remember the show *The Wonder Years* with Fred Savage, he was pretty much like me. We even had the same wavy hair. This bike was awesome. I was able to lift the front end up and use the handlebars to do sometimes the most balanced wheelies one could ever do. After school, we would get off the bus, come inside, eat some snacks, maybe watch some TV, or do some homework.

When Dad would come home, that was when we would get to the table and eat dinner together. My father was a big man. He was about six feet three and a half 240 pounds in his prime. I used to look at him and marvel at his strength. He used to run through the woods with a tree stump in his arms. Even now at this writing, he's still here, and he's still strong but much older now; he's almost eighty. He still has his strength, he still has his wisdom, and he still looks good. My mother is also older, but she still looks good and has all her mental capacity. These were the people who brought us up and made sure we knew and understood God. My mother was so protective too. Sometimes I would say I grew up under a rock, a rock of protection from my mother, but on that rock, Jesus, which is the church, was founded.

Speaking of protection, an accident almost happened to me on that Apache banana-seat bike. I was about eight or nine years old and was heading down our street Golden Brook Road when I get to the stop sign right before the fastest road near us. I stopped, I looked left, and then I looked right. I got ready to go and headed out, and as I went, this light blue Cadillac Eldorado came out of nowhere. All

I remember was seeing the left-side headlights on my left as I gave a power stroke to the pedal right toward the duck pond across the street in front of the dairy farm. I then turned quickly as adrenaline was kicking, and I was blitzing down the road at amazing speeds. The car screeched to a halt as it turned and hit the Golden Brook Road street sign. Yet another casualty to our road was that street sign. It was always getting hit or stolen.

I pedaled back to where my brother was playing with our neighbor in the woods. They were making trails. I said, "I just almost got hit by a car!" They did not believe me. I said, "Go look down there." Sure, enough we all walked out enough to see the car disabled on the side. Here was when we saw God's protection of me. This was one of the first attempts the enemy tried taking my life away. I believe I had numerous near vehicle accidents. However, they were parent-driven. No, make that three more times. I was a pre-K in Alabama when the door almost pulled me out of the car while turning in for drop-off. Those Buick Regals were something. There was a blizzard of '78 on a bridge in town, and we spun out.

Then there was that time when I fell off in the back of a truck and blacked out, when we were going to a Sunday night church service. An angel was there to protect me from the Cadillac Eldorado. I know this because there was no way it could have been just me. I saw a headlight by my rear tire. That's how close it was. This driver was the son of the lady who was in the car. He was very heavily set, fat even, and his mother had red hair, and she of course was small and feeble. I suppose he was in a rush to get her to where she was going.

I was so shaken up after that. I went home and told my parents. They took care of me. Then the police came. This police officer would approach me, and I was really shaking at this point, and he could see this and said it was not my fault and asked if I was okay. He was very tall, and that hat cocked forward made him look even taller. Then he began to question how I proceeded, and I told him exactly what I did. I looked left, nothing; right, nothing; and I started out, and there was a car. He must have been running sixty to eighty to make that distance in such a short time. The mother of the driver thought I was one of the white ducks over by the pond as I had a white T-shirt on. The driver later then proceeded to try and sue us for damages, but he was at fault. It went nowhere. He even listed my older brother since he was of age instead of me to get some money. The world is evil. This was the first lifesaving intercession in the physical world. It's truly amazing how I could have been paralyzed or dead at this point.

So you're asking this question, when did I come to know Jesus as my personal savior, as you're reading this now? That's a good question. Let's go back a bit in time to when I came to know Jesus Christ. I was just about four years old when I heard about what I was—full of sinful ideas and not perfect. Granted I was very young in life, but we are all born separated from God since the fall of Adam and Eve. It was during a vacation Bible school at Grace Baptist on July 1978.

This church was very family-oriented and used classic, fundamental, nondenominational preaching. Basically, this means they preach from the Bible and take it at its literal meaning. There was this lady from New Mexico who was a missionary who came to our church during the summer during a program called vacation Bible school. She would tell a story about God's love and what he has done for us through history.

Now I couldn't remember the story, but I do remember walking back because my brother probably walked back, and I followed my brother in whatever he did. But right then and there, I remember the color of the chairs at the back of the church before the opening that led to the congregation down the center aisle. These chairs were made of wood. They had red leather covering the cushion of the chair, typical. We used to think of these chairs as king's and queen's chairs. There was also a black railing with twisted metal bars for strength and support to keep people from falling down the stairs. This was where the coats and jackets were hung up. Remember those hangers that don't come off and make too much noise when you needed to use them? The missionary lady took us back there and explained everything to us about why we need to accept Him as our savior and how Jesus lived His life without sin, how He gave up His position of where He was physically for a time so that we could have all our sins and burdens be forgiven through His death on the cross. He died the death that we should have died to give us the life we don't deserve. Also, Jesus arose again on the third day on Easter morning just as He said He would, and just as it was prophesized over the scriptures in the Old and the New Testament. I asked Jesus in my heart. I asked Him to save me not because I've done a lot of wrong things at such a small and young age, but because I knew I was not good and feared being separated from Him forever.

We are going to take a brief time out here. I need to get through some thoughts. First and foremost, a life without Christ is pure insanity. I don't know how anyone can go through this world with everything going on without faith in God. I know in the end we will win. I will reign with Christ forever. My passion for Him, truth, is never-ending. I am bringing this here for you as time is short. Real short. This may not even make press time.

Another item of discussion is the sinner's prayer. People are now bringing it up on social media that nowhere in the Bible does it mention that prayer, only to be born again. Friends, regardless if it is written or not, you must make a decision anyway. I think what people are saying is that if we make the decision, then we are lofty and boastful. Not true. Not all people and all hearts are this way. If you keep it simple, you can see that I am a perfect example of being saved at a young age because of my acknowledgment and fear of God. I didn't save myself; I took the cue that God gave me and ran to Him. That is not predestination; that is free will—choosing to suffer with Christ now for a life with Him later forever. It is written that Moses chooses to suffer with the people of Israel and then enjoy the pleasures of sin for a season in Egypt.

> By faith Moses, when he was come to years, refused to be called the son of Pharaoh's daughter; Choosing rather to suffer affliction with the people of God, than to enjoy the pleasures of sin for a season; Esteeming the reproach of Christ greater riches than the treasures in Egypt: for he had respect unto the recompence of the reward. (Hebrews 11:24–25)

Do you see that natural tingling inside you to do right when you want to do wrong? Follow that. Do not ignore that. So again, it's not because of me. I just decided earlier than most and did not depart from that way one bit. It has been difficult, and you will read I was driving my parents crazy with no girl for a while. Stay busy, my friends. Make that money, work that dream, stop, help people, and enjoy along the way.

Now back to the wonder years. It was then here we were raised in this church. We went to Sunday school and church, and we also went to club meetings on Wednesdays. Now to top all that, sometimes we also did Christian service assignments on Saturdays. These Christian service assignments were things that we did for elderly people or the underprivileged to help them. We would do things like rake leaves, read or sing to them, and sometimes possibly bring them more meals. This was what helped develop our ability to have compassion and empathy for people.

This was me. This was my world and my life. I had to face battles in school such as the stories mentioned earlier about two of my bullies. I was just so average. I mean I did have a few special features about me. I had wavy hair when I was a kid, but as you know, most kids with wavy or curly hair have it gone when they get older, and such is the case now.

I could run, and I could play games, but the issue with my eyes that cannot be corrected even by LASIK surgery prevented me from being good in basketball or soccer. I would try out for the teams in grade school, but I did not make the basketball team. I ended up being a manager in the sixth grade which basically means picking up the balls and the pennies and making sure everything got put away, making sure that the players got on the bus, and during the away games making sure that I wrote down exactly where they shot from and if they made it. I would circle their number, and if they didn't make it, I would just leave it without being circled for statistics.

We got a good coach who played hard and worked even harder with us on our basketball skills. My next oldest brother was an all-natural jock. He could pick up any ball or tennis racket and just play. He could dunk the basketball in high school with two hands frontward or backward. In high school, he would beat every single person who was on the basketball team one on one. He even beat one of the state's number-one tennis players. As for tennis, he never really practiced much. He played a little bit because we had a neighbor who was a doctor across the street who would let us walk through the field and play on his tennis courts.

Those were the good old days. Hot summer days. So hot you could hear the bugs humming and making noise by the powerlines. Wimbledon would have their rounds of tennis being played while we were home from school. We would turn on the TV and watch tennis in the morning then get outside and either ride our bikes or play badminton and pretend that we were Wimbledon players. This was when my brother became so great in sports. My brother's name is David. He is the one that's closest to me in age. Not only was he good at sports, but he was also very smart in high school. He would never show up for any of his classes on time and just show up for the exams and pass the exams. This frustrated the teachers. So I guess you could say we were all gifted with the use of our minds.

What did I do to help cope with so much anger, hostility, and resentment toward me? I read the Bible. We did this a lot growing up in devotions with my family, my Word of Life family, or just myself. I'd often read the book of Revelations during sermons that I did not understand because I liked the end of the book. Here is what God did for me:

> As newborn babes, desire the sincere milk
> of the word, that ye may grow thereby: If so be
> ye have tasted that the Lord is gracious. (1 Peter
> 2:2–3)

Now the trick to memorizing this verse is to look at this like a child. Really, it's what we are, and this is a glimpse of how my mind worked. Now of course while writing this, I thought it was from the book of James for a second, but it was from 1 Peter. Think of a child trying to count or even say a verse. They may stumble or stutter and say, "1 Peter 2:2–3," when they mean "2:3." So that is how I remembered that one, and it gives us insight into understanding that we need to start on the simple truths and promises of God before we start going for meatier sections of the Bible.

I tell you the truth that even my hometown church did not know everything that I know now or have gained in the past two to three years in my forties. Knowledge is exploding at great magnitude as things are being revealed. Here, let me share with you a poem to encourage you as you start your walk with God. This book doesn't have all the answers, but, through experience, you may benefit from my reactions to the actions I faced.

Inspired by 1 Peter 2:2–3 and what Jesus did for us on the cross.

First Love

A love so rich and pure
How it puts a newborn's tears to rest
Quickly the babe's trust is reassured
That in time is grown to test
Time is truth in measure given
That counts the years in love of one.
Him who gave love is always within
Seeking whom for which it was done.

CHAPTER 3

My Brother's Shadow

Now you'll understand the greatness in sports and in personality that my brother David had. David was taller and stronger, and I would have to say more well-received by people. When we would go to our teenage events, and if he wasn't there with me, people would ask, "Hey, how are you doing? How is your brother?" Everyone was always concerned with David instead of me. This was another challenge in my life. I had bullies with whom I had to put up, and I had a brother who could have been drafted for a sport probably, and I was in his shadow. Yes, he was good at sports, and he tried to help me be good at sports too. He did work with me on that.

Going to church and social events after church, my brother was the life of the party. Standing by mentally while semi-engaged physically and whatever activities were going on, I could just always see how people liked him so much and not me. Growing up, we played King of the Hill, some wrestling, and athletic games, or did exercises and a lot of things together. People were just naturally drawn to him and he was older and more mentally mature, and I think that's probably where he made the greatest gains. In camp or in even Sunday school, all the girls liked him. This is what drove me a little crazy of course. I was somewhat good-looking, but my looks were always put behind under my glasses.

We would go to camp at Word of Life which really does exist and is in Schroon Lake New York. Within two hours after arriving, during the summer camp, he was wearing this pink polo shirt with khaki shorts. He had this dark tan cause he always worked outside, and his hair parted to the side, kind of like that skater bowl cut. The girls would just look at him and giggle and talk and smile, and I had to stand there and count within two hours after arriving that there were fifteen girls who made note of who he was. Obviously, this would drive me crazy because I liked girls too, of course, but it just never worked out well in the state where we lived. I would get more attention out of the state than in the state where we lived. Remember this as there is God's providence at work later in my life surrounding this. The number of years in waiting till the one came will astound you. So my brother's shadow reached far over me so much that I started to grow and cut my hair like his and parted to the side like him. I would try and wear clothes like him. This was me from 1989 to 1991. This is definitely envy fully grown. There is something that happened in that time frame that changed me, and it happened at the Word of Life island. A very special island as they say.

Trying to break out of my brother's shadow was not easy, but there were people in the church who helped me become who I am today. You will never believe what I went through during my first stay away from home with other guys in the cabin. It was very challenging. I was and am a very picky or particular person, also known as uptight. I had to share a shower and sleeping quarters with other guys. I had peculiarities that seemed to give and raise suspicion among the people with whom I bunked. Some understood and let it go; others did not. There always seems to be an antagonist in my life somewhere whether it be a bully in school or a very trying teenager in my cabin area or some situation.

For the most part, it was pretty much uneventful. However, I did have my encounters and personality conflicts as everybody does, but I was just looking to have these things to be over. I had enough of the bullies at school. I had enough of a reputation that wasn't bad but was perceived by bullies and others as something odd or strange. This was what was burning inside of me. This was what consumed me. This was what created increased levels of anger and hate including rage. Oh, yes. Don't get me wrong. Remember that even as a child of God, I'm not perfect, and I am still a sinner, but I'm just forgiven.

There were times up there at Word of Life when I had it in for someone. Our first year working at Word of Life was at the Island in 1990. It didn't matter the location as I was always in his shadow in his presence. You know the same thing still played out. "Hey, where's your brother?" seemed to be most of my communication with other people. I felt like Cain, and he was Abel. Am I my brother's keeper? Don't get me wrong. My brother was an antagonist to me too at home, and we would fight. Don't you worry about that? He got to me at some point; it escalated so greatly that I was going after my brother with such anger. I didn't want to hurt him, but he angered me and would not leave me alone. I think it was when I went for a baseball bat that he changed his mind. That was the end of his antagonistic ways. No, I did not hurt him.

Word of Life Island 1990 was, great and I learned a lot. I saw a lot as I grew inside as well as outside because I was only sixteen. I was able to be more talkative since we didn't have many other things to do than talk or play, and I think that helped me make connections with people. I saw value in that, and they saw value in me. Some things just happened there that were not supposed to happen. They were not bad things, and these bonds are physical contact like holding hands or putting an arm around someone. I made these connections happen. It was a rule at Word of Life not to touch girls or walk into town without a third party, or you would get written up. I must have broken that rule on accident and on purpose so many times. This was good for me as it helped build confidence, and nature would take over—controlled and respectful nature that is, and for the most part.

You change the most when you are uncomfortable.

You change the most when you are uncomfortable. That statement is very true. I was out of my element and in another place. The separation was hard at first, but as time went on, I grew to like it. There are some things you know you need, and there are things you know you can do without. That mental process of thinking is the learning moment. I soon realized that I could be away from home and be alright. The next part was learning to deal with people and personalities.

Separation anxiety for home is real. The first week or two was really tough. I was looking for a safety net so scheduling and patterns were what I was looking for. There were days I could call home, and there were days I could be me without being supervised. I looked forward to mail days, as like everyone else, I wanted to hear from home. The best were the care packages we'd get. They'd send things up, and we'd get to eat some things that reminded us of home. It also gave room for people to steal from us as well. There was no real privacy there, and that was one of the things that really gets under my skin. Then the personalities came out. Some people were there because they wanted to be, some were sent, and some should have never come. I see a lot of patterns in this review myself as at the end of the days, there would be apostasy, a falling away, and there would be very secular or worldly Christians who are really not. This microcosm in Upstate New York is the same thing as what I was thirty-one years ago. Yes, that clock is ticking.

There was one girl there who wanted to save me from being in my brother's shadow. She knew me from childhood and saw in me something that I didn't see. She was Erin. You won't believe how a teenage boy would cry after getting his hair cut by a girl. It did happen, and it was me. My anchor or defensive object or my sense of security was my ability to look like something that works and wins which was my brother's image. His shadow was so great that I created a mold of me representing him in some way.

Erin was a local girl from her hometown who loved the Lord and had a gift of music and singing. She was always competing at Word of Life in the singing competition or in creative writing. Interestingly enough, I did not compete in creative writing but look at me now and this book—who knew? She was very talented and beautiful. Her voice like is that of an opera singer at times. She watched and witnessed all the things that I had to experience being the younger sibling. She knew; she was the older sibling in her family. However, as girls, I don't think it was the same as it was with my brother.

As the scissors came out, and the hair was falling, tears fell on both sides of my face. I had to trust the process. It was a difficult fifteen minutes, but in the end, I was better off. My hair was naturally wavy and curly. We gelled it up, and that was the look—the wet look of curly hair and preppy clothes. This was the new me, and I was proud of it, maybe too much as some would say, but there were some who years later told me the entire girls' cabin including counselors said I was a good catch. Right? I could have used that information earlier in my life, like that summer! Yes, it's always good to hear reaffirming compliments.

This marked the beginning of my ability to form my own identity. And I think it's very important that people develop themselves fully to be sure of themselves and to be confident. The self-worth that you have inside from what you do as challenges and successes or failures helps create the person that you are today. I was growing up, and this was one of my first experiences of identifying who I was period.

Now in the '90s, we did not have any gender or equality issues that made the news. The '80s and '90s were the best at least from a teenage boy's point of view. I am sure there were issues but out of my world. I would count myself fortunate to have grown up in the '80s. While I didn't know all the intent of all the music and everything that's out there, it sounded good; it was happy and bubbly. Between the '80s and the '90s and high school, I had wants and dreams and desires. I was able to dream of something I wanted in the future and have desires and believed I could achieve this.

While writing this book, life had been a struggle even though I know I was struggling less than others. I had forgotten what I wanted. It's almost as if I must find more of the things I love to do because I work so much. I think it's very important for people to identify who they are to feel comfortable in their skin and have confidence. Through interactions with other people—sports and life—I think we would be able to develop sound foundations. We know this isn't possible for everyone.

If you're reading this book now, and you may have come from a broken home, maybe a home that's plagued with violence, hate, envy, jealousy, drug addiction, alcohol, or any other addictions, it is extremely hard to understand the life that you can have. I want you to know while you're reading this book, that my life was not a silver spoon handed to me. Even though we came from different walks of life, it doesn't mean you can't have the same thing either or that the journey is any different. It's different based on circumstances, but we are all imperfect and sinful and are looking to make it better for ourselves and the ones we love. It's not a bunch of buzzwords and sunshine talk. But everything begins in the mind.

Every thought, every sin, and every action begins there. If you can master your thoughts, you will be successful. Your thoughts are the initiators and workhorses to where you are now in life from two or three years ago. Your decisions are your only chance. Read that again. Therefore, it is important to make good, sound decisions and surround yourself with like-minded, positive people and people who are even better than you. I'm not saying to surround yourselves with fans. Surround yourselves with people who are better than you at something, not necessarily at something you can do but something that you admire that you are trying to master. Learn from them, share with them, and create that dynamic in the exchange.

So there went 1990. In 1991, my brother and I both went to work at an inn. This was great because we were no longer waterlocked by the lake. We could get out and do things. You must remember the rules at Word of Life where if you go with a girl somewhere, you must bring a third person with you. There had to be no touching. This was a very weird and strange type of behavior, although I understand its intention. I think it was not good, not because I had problems those days with touch or emotion but because I wanted to be a little bit more engaging and empathetic and emotional to the ones I love.

Don't get me wrong. We broke the rules even when we didn't know we were breaking the rules because some things just weren't natural. I got a few demerits walking into town with a girl. It happens. Nothing bad happened because I memorized scripture. I knew the hot buttons, and I knew where the cold water was, for example.

In 1991, things started to change. Things started to go my way. Just like the island when I was out of state and out of my normal confines, the labels and restrictions that my childhood environment brought upon me were gone. I was somebody else. I was still in high school, and in fact, one time during high school, I think it was probably during my junior year, I was sucker punched. I had been corrected for talking to someone's girlfriend and welcoming her to campus. I'd call this person bully number 4.

As for bully number 3, we didn't really cover them in grade school, but we probably saw more of him in high school too but freshman year, and his name is Karl. Karl was bitter, self-centered, and righteous in his own mind. He didn't like God. He had it out for him, and he didn't really understand how I thought the way I did. Whenever he would talk to me, he would engage me with such animosity that it was almost as if I were disgusting to him. Karl at the time of this writing died. I don't know what happened to him, and I did not wish death upon him, not even at the time when he would make fun of me or tag along with other people to ridicule me or pick apart anything that I tried to stand for Jesus. I knew this was the price of being a Christian.

Bully number 4 was Pete. Pete sucker punched me on the high school campus.

Here was how that went. In high school, I was not good at math and was taking consumer math or business math, and we had a new student come in. This student looked like she got her finger stuck in an outlet, literally 1980 hair band girl with the big poof. I was nice though, and when I and the guys were coming back from lunch off campus, we said hello and went back to class. The next day or so, as our bus pulled up to let the town kids off, we stood up before the bus went to a complete stop as was customary, and I looked out the window. I noticed something different. There was a crowd of people, and in the crowd, I saw her, that new girl. You couldn't miss her, that hair and those green eyes. Well, next to her was a boy, and he looked like he was on a mission.

This was post-summer 1991 when I thought I met the girl of my dreams from Fort Wayne, Indiana. Keep this in mind. As I walked off the bus and headed to homeroom, the boy said, "Hey, you!" I turned around and said hi and then he just started talking, feeding himself into a frenzy in his mind. "You hitting on my girl?" said Pete. I said no and that I was just being nice and greeting her to the school like the other two guys I was with. I was sure to mention two other guys and continued to walk to homeroom.

Apparently, that wasn't enough. I then told him I have a girlfriend and was not pursuing her like he thought. Well, that didn't go well as he was looking to prove himself at my expense. "What? My girl's not good enough?" Pete stated as he was moving around a bit more physically looking for an opportunity to strike.

I said, "No, that's not what I meant. I'm all set." I turned away at that moment, and that was when he punched me. At least I was walking away, so it wasn't so bad. I turned and looked at him, touched my bloody lip, and walked to the nurse's office.

I remember one bystander, a Hispanic boy saying, "He got you good." Later on in life, I saw Mr. Pirez in the dentist's office, and boy did he age. I reminded him of the story, and he remembered. Just recanting the old days while waiting to be seen. The school eventually pressed charges against him for the assault even if I didn't. Note that his father was a marine, and when he got home, he got taken care of. Later on in life, at the time of this writing, Pete is also dead. Pete died of kidney cancer.

I did not wish anything bad on Pete either. In fact, after the incident, he called me up and apologized and I said, "Yeah, no worries, man." I was just being a welcome wagon to his girlfriend and being friendly. We laughed and had a few chuckles, and I was like, "Hey, I wish you the best." I suppose his girlfriend just wanted attention, and this was one way to get it. I had a girlfriend at the time whom I met at Word of Life. I thought I was going to marry her. We met at a camp for two weeks and had a relationship long distance for almost two years. It never happened as I never got the guts to drive out to see Jamie in Fort Wayne, Indiana.

Jamie was a volleyball player standing five feet seven, with long brown hair, a defined jaw line, and deepest of blue eyes, and she was a ton of hometown, letterman-jacket-wearing charm. Picture her like someone from the *Smallville* TV show, like Lana. Yes, I thought she was it. Our song was Amy Grant's "I Will Remember You." I used to light right up hearing that. We had songs for each other. Heck, we used to make tapes for each other with the songs and meanings. I might actually still have it. Yes, it was high school puppy love as I was never able to man up and make the drive. Too much of a mama's boy and that I never thought I'd get as far as I was to go. I used to look into so many emotions, feelings, and signs that we were to be together. There were many, but that's almost like idolatry looking for readings and signs if you let it get the best of you. Although I look for them now in other ways, it's a more mature way where God talks to me and not looking for wet ground and dry fleece. I'm sure she's fine now. She's married and has two kids the last I checked.

So where were we? Ah yes, the time in the summer of 1991 was great. I ended up meeting some people having fun playing volleyball during the day and washing dishes at night. It's kind of funny. You don't know this, but each time I worked up there at Word of Life, I was washing dishes and now I know why God was preparing me to be a dishwasher in my house. I thought you might laugh.

1991 was good because I did so many things besides helping with wave runner rentals at the beach during the day and playing volleyball. I got to meet some cool people and a few girls along the way and some interesting characters.

During this time, I was accepted, I was highly desirable, and things were going a boy's way. I didn't cross the line. We may have turned the heat on a bit here and there, but nothing ever happened. I was too smart for that situation and wouldn't allow it. Some people made mistakes in their lives at Word of Life. But I held on to virtue and integrity in mine. I never sacrificed the one thing that I could not get back. I know some people think it's so old-school, but I think there's a reason why, and for some people more than others, you just don't give it away. Don't get me wrong. Even today I must be careful. The eye gate to the soul and the wonder of our mind must be carefully guarded. Fifteen minutes of fun or the forty-eight seconds, I need just doesn't add up to all the heartbreak it would cause.

The Bible holds the relationship between men and women of the sexual kind in high regard. It is where two become one, and they leave their parents. It also manifests and emulates the Trinity because a man and a woman married walking with God have a relationship with God. I got this from Jimmy Evans who does the Tipping Point broadcast on YouTube. He makes a great point that Satan was not interested in Adam until Eve showed up. Why, you ask. They represented the Trinity. That is why God created man in His own image and created Eve to be with Adam as a helper. Satan has been attacking God's design since the day Eve showed up. So are you ready for a story? I bet you are.

One day, up in the Adirondacks, I took out a Pontiac LeMans with a friend and learned, or should I say, started to learn how to drive. Correct. A Pontiac LeMans I think was from the '70s, and it was big, and back then, metal was heavy. So imagine a seventeen-year-old driving a car full of girls and another guy to the mall at Glens Falls—yes, that long road Route 9, and at times I was swerving. I was trying to take the emblem of the Pontiac and place it on the white line as a guide to keep the car in the correct lane. This thing was a boat. It was amazing I went and drove and did well. A friend who was there was very kind and gracious enough to trust me with driving with the lives of other people in the car. You won't see this today with the laws going on now and of course with the onset of the phone. It was a good time.

I was dating a girl at that time, and she was half Chinese and half American, and her name was Jen. That relationship lasted for about two weeks. Time was both fast and slow. In two weeks, out of ten made it feel like a month when you were dating. Strangely enough as good as she looked, she never thought she'd be the person who wanted to talk about God. That was one of the reasons she broke up with me was due to not talking about God. I didn't get that perception of what she wanted with how she carried herself or what she said. No worries. There are more fish in the sea, and sure enough, another week I had another girlfriend. While at Word of Life, dating wasn't as dating is; and in a limited capacity, we did the best we could. I did meet Jaime later on in this summer as mentioned earlier. So I was walking on the rays of the sun at this point.

So here I was, and that concluded this summer. There were many outings and fun and things of that nature, and this was the last year that my brother was with me and did this summer camp. You know what this meant for me, right? Not only did I have to come out of my shell and out of the shadow, but now it was just me. My brother was going to go to Word of Life Bible Institute after high school, and he did, and I think he was working elsewhere at the time to get money to go. He later met his wife at Word of Life, so the saying goes. The rest was history for him. He did some things out of sequence, which we were taught not to do but, in the end, life evens up for all of us. It's best to wait and get your career sorted out, but I guess even my parents didn't either, and that's news at the time of this writing with them being eighty and me almost fifty. I was the only one in the family to get a degree and then a master's degree in time.

CHAPTER 4

I Know My Stuff

Well, as you can see, I have been put through a lot of theological training and educational training. I have scored decently in school and rather very high spiritually. I had CliffNotes to life by reading the Bible. It was my key to success, but at this young age, I was looking for shortcuts. Hey, I know my stuff, right?

Being full of pride and arrogance was something that really emanated from me. There were two reasons: dealing with my brother's shadow syndrome (I call it that) and knowing what was coming and the end. So what did God do for me? At this point in life, I was at college-age, but I was not really going to college. I decided to take a break from school and just work full-time. Life and the devil took me for a ride. It's not a bad ride, not the ones that probably are bestsellers, but as I have mentioned, the average Joe perspective. I started working in a fast-food place full-time and then went on to a warehouse. I had some temptations of the opposite sex a few times. Luckily, I came out unscathed. What was it that held me together? All the teachings of my youth. However, I was playing with fire. I am not going to go into details, but there is nothing new under the sun, as King Solomon once said, as well as there is nothing new under covers either.

Please pardon the fast-tracking of details and stories, but what is important here that I want to take the time to share is the Holy Spirit pricking one's conscience about one's activities. Yes, that little voice inside your head that makes you feel bad about what you are doing really was sounding some gongs to me. In one instance, I thought someone was in the room or in my head, and I did hear a sigh, and a groan, as I was grieving the Holy Spirit. Jesus will never take you into a situation that far exceeds your ability to withstand. However, you must have the mind to bring every thought to the obedience of Christ.

> Casting down imaginations and every high thing that exalteth itself against the knowledge of God and bringing into captivity every thought to the obedience of Christ. (2 Corinthians 10:5)

This means to bring everything in alignment with the view of the King of kings for your life. Everything starts in the mind, from good ideas to bad. When you start to feel insecure or unsure or proud and boasting, maybe when you want to do something sinful or bad, you must stop to realize and ask, "Is this something God would approve of?" Should I even have these thoughts, or should I let the battle in the spiritual realm be given over to God? We must have disciplined thought. It's so hard.

Grace and mercy are gifts from the Father for eternal life with Him. Accepting that is easy once you want to and come to the knowledge of His saving grace. Now this is the hard part—living for the Lord. This is where lofty thoughts or lies can take precedence and then make you act down that wrong path. Say you have some need to be accepted or popular. You need to be with that hottest guy or girl to be where you think you need to be. STOP. Those are the lies of the devil trying to get you to fall. Satan is not just going to come out and put you directly and immediately in a sinful situation. No, he is the great deceiver and will sow seeds of doubt and fear as though you might miss out on something if you don't do it. The oldest tricks in the book are suspicion, doubt, and fear.

How do we act against these thoughts? Great question, and I am so glad you asked. Memorization of key verses of the Bible verse helps with the struggle in life. Also we can focus on Christ's victory over sin and death. Once you come to know Christ and start walking with Him, you need to read and apply as well as surround yourself with people who will hold you accountable and keep you pushing hard through life's troubles and temptations.

In the end, you will be better for it. Remember, this life is a test, a game of life, and is temporary. You already have the upper hand being made in the image of Christ and most favored among all creation. Why do you think the devil tries so hard to disrupt that? He's not worried about the fallen people who actively reject Jesus and are sinful; he already owns them. He is looking to make Christians stumble and fall to poke holes in the faith and cause even more to give up hope. This is the very reason why this book is about you and the purpose of the Ancient of Days. You are the *I* in "I am God's dream."

Okay, well, that was a compressed, accelerated segment, but what else happened in the years following high school? I worked in fast food—McDonald's. Food, folks, and fun! It was probably one of the best times of my life—from getting my first job, buying my first car, and having a social life. There was not much chance of anything socially happening in that small town. It was like Whoville where the Grinch came to steal Christmas from. There was not much going on in my small town, and the social life there was extremely limited. At times, I felt like I was driving thousands of miles searching for friends and nightlife but never found it. I didn't. I even forced bad relationships to happen just not to be lonely. How does one do this, you say? Hanging around people who are not a good influence and have poor self-actualization of themselves for starters. Poor self-esteem and addiction plagued many of the larger *rural* city kids. Also, they would be looking for that pseudo-grand lifestyle. It all comes down to parenting. Read that again, and you will see this in a lot of the problems we face now as well as then.

Then entered a small-city girlfriend from a semi-large high school. Yeah, I thought hanging out with seniors and being on a date for a prom was the thing to do. They ended up taking my money for the limo rental and booze and leaving without me. I was being used but was looking for attention. It was not good. Nothing happened, and God made sure of that, but these people were so conceited and narcissistic that even the guy's mother was wearing my Shaquille O'Neal shirt when I went to pick it up. So messed up. It was keeping up with the Joneses to have the best. Later I learned that my date puked her brains out and was an alcoholic. She was to waste her youth on that bottle.

As you can see, this episode, after getting a car and trying to be with the crowd, wasn't so exciting. I was warned but did that one date and learned. I went back to doing laps around several towns as I drove myself through the boredom. What was God really doing here? My brother met his wife and got married early. Heck, he is even a grandpa now (middle brother). I was upset more at being alone than getting burned.

I had to do this a few more times before I realized I needed to head to the sea and change my crowd. I did. I found some volley-ball-loving people at the water where money and opportunity were more abundant, and that trailer-park lifestyle and mindset were long forgotten. Hope was restored, but still, I was a little lonely. Please understand that labels and stereotypes are used for illustrations and not judgment. Back in the day, I was fire-and-brimstone judgmental and supercritical because of some overprotective parenting and female bravado commando protection over my life, my mom! Only when I got married to this wonderful Eastern European gal did I finally see how much of a jerk I can be or I was.

So here we have a White male from the small-town USA, a Bible-beating, fire-and-brimstone preaching, and super knowledgeable and energetic youth driving nonbelieving people most likely away from Christ than to Christ. I know my stuff, and I had all the big issues covered. Drugs, sex, alcohol, laziness, being unemployed, etc. we're not part of me. I was Superman Jr. and ready to trot. Slow down, Kal-El, right? God provided opportunities for me to test my willpower and discipline as well as show me what life is like when empty. Only sounds eerily familiar in a recent *Superman* movie where Jor-El wanted Kal-El to know what it was like to be weak and human. Searching for like-minded Christian youth and those who wanted to call you back and bring you it was difficult. I lived twenty-two miles up the road and had to commute to new friends.

I learned a lot that God was bringing couples together, and life was taking off for them. I thought maybe I'd have a chance with a beauty, but that didn't pan out. Then it happened. Seven years later after debacle (but not really) number X, I met my wife. Yes, can you believe how this stuff works out? Note the years seven years in between. I never really knew it to be a season, but now I am seeing others post-marriage and divorce and talking about being in a season of waiting. I realize now that I have been there and done that. It was no fun and not easy on the human spirit. My parents went bonkers listening to me complain and ask, "Where is she?" On August 6, 2004, a Wednesday, I took my future wife out on a first date.

We met at a local casino where she was working the cash register at the gas station, and I was working the surveillance cameras and fixing them. A colleague and I drove up to check out the camera and the Polish girl. We had a bet going on about who would be the first one to score a date with these H1B travel visa holders. Guess what? I won. Her eyes were blue and on fire. I had to duck as I got close to the register as the blue eyes were fire to me. Her friend was an older lady who was a matchmaker and asked me if I wanted to go on a date. I said sure. I wasn't going to not say anything and spineless. So I went up to her and asked if she wanted to go for a ride on a motorcycle and hit the beach. She said yes. I was totally stoked, as they say. Interesting what played out next over a few times together. Since she worked so much, I'd hang out with her while she was watching the store at the mall. I really had no idea what I was getting into. I was just following that heart light.

Days passed between dates, and we really started to get to know each other more. Our first date was at my place. I believe it was dinner and a movie. She liked watermelon, and we watched that mermaid movie. I can remember the futon we were on as I think she spilled the watermelon. She's a believer before God, but I think her culture branded a few stories that everyone goes to heaven and not to use your faith. Yeah, as weird as those sounds. It does not mean to not believe in God, but I don't believe they actively put their trust in God daily or talked daily with Him.

I'm going to be the first to say this right now. She is the most peaceful and caring person one can be. She was a little shy, whereas I was brought up under fire-and-brimstone days and Bible-smashing unbelievers for being ignorant or unwilling. So what really happened was that, in my life, I got all the big things right—saved, walking the walk, staying clean, etc., not sinning, but I was brutally honest and sometimes mean. I confess I did not know how I was perceived till I met this lovely European flower. It has taken years to refine me, peeling back layers and years of tough skin from an overly critical, judgmental, and always-right mother. Does this mean there is peace in my heart, and I was a somewhat decent human? Of course, but it's those little things they say, and so it seems to me. Anyway, I just wanted to give you some insight there. No believer is ever perfect. We are all the same, just forgiven. Also, our desires are not to sin or displease the Father but to walk in the path He has for us. Some have been put through a ton of Biblical learning and application on the big items, but because of stress, they may snap at the small things of lesser consequence.

On our second date, I think it was a ride on the bike out to my parent's place. Yes, on the second date, meet the parents. Well, after what I mentioned in the previous paragraph, she must meet some nice people, right? Watch it! Kidding. That was a dinner there, and my brother was over as well with his first wife at the time. It was all good and we have photos. Then came the third date. This I remember as it was Italian night, and we had calzones. It was on this third date that I felt she was the one. Almost like my predecessors (my parents) who knew on their third date they were meant for each other.

The third date was at Illiano's Calzones, and we watched two movies which in one, we talked more than did anything else. *Dirty Dancing* and *Ghost* were the two feature films that she liked. This was where the truth came out. A lot happened here on this date, and I will get into that next.

Illiano's is one of those places that just bring you into the restaurant. Freshly baked bread and dough were always being mingled with tomato sauce. As we walked in, all eyes went straight to my Polish girlfriend and me as they always do. We placed our order and then walked over to Blockbuster to rent two movies. These two movies had been something of her favorites for all time. One was *Dirty Dancing*, and the other was *Ghost*. She loved the storyline in each of these films. I was more than happy to be her dance partner for life.

When we got back to Illiano's, we stood outside the door because our calzones were not ready yet. It was at this time I found out that she did not like black olives. "More for me," was all I have to say. Standing outside, she said the most outstanding statement I have ever heard on the third date.

She said, "When we have children, promise me that if they do not like something, you will not force them to eat it."

I said, "Sure, honey, I will never do that."

Then I asked her, "What made you say something like that? Were you ever forced to eat something you didn't like?" She said no. Shocking as it sounded, I was wondering when we decided to become a formal couple. I didn't hear anything official. I liked it very much to hear her say "I love you." It had been spoken, and we had announced our dreams aloud to each other almost publicly declaring them as prayers. So I was happy and content that she was content with me as a person to whom she could say those things. After this, I was the only one in the world. I felt so blessed that this kindhearted person loved me so much that she would consider me a good father. I am honored to be considered for such a role. I am happy and over-joyed to have her as my wife forever.

We proceeded to take the calzones and the movies back to my place. As soon as we got in, I was clearing the table to prepare a place for her and me to sit and eat. I began to pray over the food and hold her hand. I was filled with so much exuberance a child has when he gets home from school to play with his friend. Here was my new friend, and she was pleasing to the eyes. We began to eat and talk about our day at work and what we like about Italian food.

One thing that was strange about her eating the calzone was the use of ketchup. I have never seen anyone use ketchup on a calzone. That would be like using A.1. Steak Sauce on a sausage for breakfast. I asked her about the reason, and it was one of those things she just liked. Later, when I visited Poland to see her, I knew the reason. A lot of the food they have is pickled or salted or something that puts a zing in your taste buds. I took her extra calamari sauce and doused the calzone and ate. Toward the end, she never finished, and I saved half of mine for us to eat on another day.

Now it was movie time. My newfound girlfriend took charge of it as it was the movies that she liked. We put in movie number one, but we were talking throughout the movie, so I did not see much of it. She said next time, I had to concentrate a little harder on the movie and not her. We had a blast talking and discovering new things about each other. Every time we are together, it just keeps getting better. A love like this can only be provided by someone who knows what they are doing. In all my writing I could not describe how intuitive this relationship has been. After watching the movies and talking for an hour after that, we were really burning the wicks here on both ends, and we called it a night. Another drive home singing, a few goodnight kisses, and a hug were about to ensue. One of the best nights of my life was this one. What we did and talked about created a pulse in the universe that felt a magnitude so grand.

That was how it all began, folks: simple, fun, and passionate. I have never known a love like this. This is one powerful relationship that I do not worry about but enjoy for a change. Little Miss Poland is the girl I've always wanted to be friends with, to party with, to grow with, and to be my mate for life. There are no words to describe this feeling. It's like pushing with all your might to describe even how her fingers touch my face gently. Innocent love is priceless. I thank You, God, for bringing her into my life. May I always do right in Your eyes with what You have given me.

I just wanted to share that portion of my life with you because waiting on God to make things happen is not easy. First, we are human and timely. We are all bound by the clock, and we do expire. Second, we are physical and tied to the flesh. Meaning, we can only experience and know what we can see and touch or relate to. So as I mentioned, a friend of mine said she was on a waiting period. This can be like Daniel from the Bible, who was waiting for years for God to do things. This was the period before I met my wife. I drove my parents nuts by asking, "Where is she? If my brother and sister got married, why am I waiting?" Yes, it's not easy, and people can make wrong and impulsive human decisions when he rests on his own power. What does God say about this?

> Trust in the LORD with all your heart
> and lean not on your own understanding;
> in all your ways submit to him,
> and he will make your paths straight. (Proverbs 3:5–6)

God is most interested in a relationship with us. He doesn't care about telling us where we went wrong. We are all born of sin and fallen since Adam and Eve. God sent His son Jesus as the real breaker of chains. Jesus lived a sinless life to die on the cross for all our sins of old and in the future. Our flesh locks in our old man's ways. Old man refers to the sin of nature we are all born with. When one accepts Christ as their Savior and has Him direct their life, they are indwelled and sealed by the Holy Spirit. This represents the Trinity of God the Father, Son (Jesus), and the Holy Spirit. Old things are passed away indwelt and all things become new. We become new creatures in Christ. This doesn't mean we start being sinless, but our desires change. When you lean on the Lord for discernment and understanding of the choices that you make, they end up being better choices.

Now what happens here to me, you ask? Why was I being paired up with a lady who was not spiritual like I was having all the Bible knowledge, memory verses, church experience, yada yada? God knew I needed refinement. He placed someone caring and loving in my midst instead of my protective and defensive/offensive mother. Don't get me wrong. I love my mother, but her past shaped her cynical approach to people and life like a cold blade of life meeting the righteous judgment of the Almighty God. The combination of having a sharp edge and the knowledge of divine judgement is like enriched Uranium in Iran. Just don't do that. I needed to be polished by a Polish girl for the smaller things in life. She slowed me down in a lot of ways, and we will get to that too later. You must stop and smell the roses as they say. Since being in my brother's shadow and being on the losing end of many competitive stakes, I just had this edge to push through everything and force things to happen.

This was just another example of how God had prepared my way before I got there. I just had to realize the door and walk through, that sometimes it is the hardest part for all of us to agree on. Our pride, our agenda, and the people or places we are in "force us" to make wrong decisions. The quotations around us force us that it's not really forcing us, but we are under the influence. That's why it's so important to surround yourself with people who will push you to greater things and have demonstrated experience.

Since we are on the topic of slowing down and letting go and letting God, God has designed us for praising Him, worshiping Him, and be in fellowship with each other as well as Him. I would like to share with you what colors in the earth God had revealed to me living in the Northeast United States. In the fall, it gets very colorful, and if you take the time to travel to Northwestern Mass in mid-October, it's really pretty. Also, New Hampshire is the place to be for leaf peeping as they call it. In college, while in a humanities class, I learned a bit about art and had to write a poem among many other projects. My inspiration was a song by Michael W. Smith, "Crystal Throne," and my New England experience as a young Christian man. Take a minute to read just how special Earth is and how we are to care for it.

The Painted Earth

The earth and sky are His canvas
Land and ocean are colors on a palette
Who moves this art and makes it last
With colors of emotion, so deep and heartfelt?

He placed it down into the soul of man
Earth, He created with just one stroke
This is the painting of the Master Artist's plan
Filled it with nature's beauty as He spoke

Who is this that bends color and light?
It is God, Jehovah, the everlasting
That makes the shapes with His might
A gift to man from God so loving

If you are ever wondering if you're just a mistake, a freak of nature, or somewhere in between, let me tell you that you are not. Psalm 139:13–14 says we are knitted together in our mother's womb and that we are fearfully and wonderfully made. God gave us all this earth to enjoy and to keep. Our senses are just a reduced capacity of what we take in down here on earth compared to what our heavenly bodies will be able to take in when we are up there. After reading this chapter, take a minute to go outside and enjoy a walk with someone and just be in conversation with the person and nature.

CHAPTER 5

The Working Years

Fast-forward to the working years before or after college and getting married. There were a lot of challenges I faced not, just financially but also career- and relationship-wise. One business tip for you while reading this book is that it's all about people in the end. If you keep that in mind, working, selling, and living come down to what people are perceiving and consuming, which then shows that this principle is derived from the Bible, the greatest business book of all time. There are a lot of truths and principles from the Bible that translate to the working world. Trust me. I am not saying reading the Bible or being a Christian will get you rich, but it will help you make do with what you have while you are here.

My first job after high school was in a fast food, and then I moved on to a warehouse where there were many battles. In the neck of the woods where I lived, jobs were very blue collar or some places were too small to hire or aspire up through the ranks. I was influenced by my parents and the news to hate city life. Yeah, pretty much right there, huh? Hate and discrimination transcend even the "Christian" households. Again, parental experience spoken to a child can be very impressionable.

Remember that the most impressionable years and where most things are taught are at ages one to twelve. My mother had some bad run-ins, and so did my father. However, we were in the '90s now, and work was work, but a few people at the warehouse were very down and out and negative. I am not saying all but only a few, and the few who frequented me were a bit much. As witness to everyone there, they kept asking why bad things happen to good people and why things happen. All I could do was point them to God's will and what He wants brought to pass.

God could flick us off the planet like ants as He has all the power and rights. One day we will find out how long He was around before He got bored and created us. This is one of the biggest questions I need to be answered. Anyway, many of the blue-collar and suffering working class asked these questions. Mind you, the work at the warehouse was hard since we were moving a lot of products. The days and life could be daunting.

There I suffered persecution for my faith in many ways. Some would get me alone and ask sincere questions. Then when around and with their friends, they'd ask questions to make fun. You can see right there that a battle would be taking place not just against me but the person inside them. They would search and look for reason and hope and were ashamed of trying. That hurtful feeling would turn its claws out and then lash out at the person trying to deliver the hope. It was also during this time that I again would try and force or believe in a relationship. It was one of the worst ever and most jarring. God got me through and out despite raging hormones. It was so tough to deny myself, pick up His cross, and leave, but the relationship wasn't healthy.

I eventually moved out of the blue-collar to white-collar while going to school. I had many coop and internships that helped cultivate business management skills and more employment opportunities.

In between all that, I had good years and some bad. Let me tell you that not everything was easy. Some of the opportunities were at the casino. I considered this my jump-off point as I was in and out of there a few times. I think three in total. First was when the HR assisted in processing new hires, and this was part of my college placement department. I did fine but again ran into a love triangle that I did not mean to cause. Nothing bad happened, and nothing really happened at all, but I never realized the impression I had on this girl until someone told me. Again, even the best of us can be influenced by our bodies, physical attraction, and old nature than the new man God has given us once we accept Jesus into our hearts. We're forgiven and not perfect. Also we should not believe we are exclusive or too good for people, as we are all on this journey. The reason for this book is for you to get the CliffNotes on life as I did but even faster.

I left the HR to do some security and surveillance work with cameras, analog, and network video. It was there that my passion for technology exploded. Let me tell you, I knew my stuff and had a hunger for more. Even today, as a successful cybersecurity expert, I live for it. The only thing that trumps my hunger for tech is reading and understanding God's word in prophecy. Everyone should be excited about what's to come. If this book ever gets out, look up as prophecy is unfolding at an alarming rate. Prophecy is one-third of the Bible.

In this new role as CCTV or CATV person, I learned everything and loved it. However, again, there were personality conflicts at the coworker and manager levels. I was so inspired by being in college that I thought I knew even more than in my teenage years. So what I call being eighteen for ten years is twenty eight. This is where I still thought I knew it all and proved it emphatically. I literally put a plan on the desk of the managers proposing the things we should do. I know now that in life, it wasn't the right thing to do. Wait, are you smirking while reading this? I am too. I should not have put a plan of what to do down on their desks as it was probably not the best way, and I think it was a little condescending. In that casino world, the mentality there was very high school and so political. I realized shortly after I left that it was just not the place for me. I was so frustrated with stupid that was going on there that I left. Remember I left two more times. Fortunately, I had a great education and learned a lot about computers and networks.

When I did leave, it was after I met my future wife. One of the hardest things to do is be responsible not only for yourself but the ones you love and the family you may one day have. Please put a mental asterisk here as we will come back "Never again," meaning unemployed. Spoken with such a resolute tone in my voice.

I left the casino to go work for a mom-and-pop computer shop. They offered to pay for my gas even when not at work. I couldn't believe it, especially when gas was not cheap. Anyway, here I was going out on a limb, leaving the casino after leaving my parents' place. So I had bills to pay, and I took this step as I was passed over for a computer/network role at the casino. It was okay for a while, but I was not getting enough billable hours, and when my clients didn't decide to go over to the mom-and-pop shop well, they said I couldn't install Windows XP to can me. Don't worry, I could install it, and the owner later got entangled in another white-collar crime years later. I'm not surprised.

There I was unemployed, engaged (that's a whole book in itself), and having bills to pay. I was really at the mercy of God looking for work in this area. After graduating in 2002, at age twenty-seven, it was hard to find work, to begin with other than the casino. So many options were considered, and I even worked as a recruiter at a school for a short time. I prayed and stayed connected with friends. I had to file for unemployment. At this time I started a computer and network consulting business. This was where I would work gigs as they came to get money flowing. It was such a process. Each week I would call in on Sunday or Monday to the unemployment office. So embarrassing, but I got used it.

This was a time when God really proved to me He is real, not just for the lifesaving, don't-want-to-go-to-hell idea when I was little. He helped when I was against all odds. One day, I went into a bike shop to get parts, and I thought I should apply for a job. I really wasn't planning on applying for a job, but as I walked in there, the manager looked at me and said, "You look like you need a job." I wish they said that after college.

In life, there are no guarantees. College is not easy or for everyone. In fact, you could say that I went to college to figure out how the world works and how people work in business. The rest, I picked up on my own. For example, one time, I was working for a small business deploying a network based on the experience I obtained on the job at the casino. Now this would be something you can't learn in school, but you can learn the concepts, and you still must apply the knowledge. Some of this knowledge is demonstrated by working with network media such as CAT5 or CAT6 cables or terminated ends on fiber optics. In this case, there was no need for fiber optics, but I had to run wiring throughout an office building to hook up computers for a physical security company. That was one opportunity I was working on while being unemployed.

I know you are at the edge of your seat. I did accept the job at the bike shop. There was no shame, and working no matter what you do there is no shame. What really got me from where I came from to where I am now is a smaller paycheck. Also, I was not working in my field or my career designation. I put my pride on the shelf and started to come to work. I also had to come to work on Saturdays and work half a day or till three o'clock. What hurt me the most—and might bring a tear to your eye while reading this—was that I was going to marry the girl of my dreams while working for a bike shop as a parts counter-person. This was so hard to take that there were times during the summer of 2005 before we were going to get married that we were having this awkward conversation. "Hello, honey. Guess what I'm doing? I'm doing parts for $10.50 an hour. Can't wait to see you come to America for the best life ever."

I would usually find myself in the storage warehouse crying or trying to hold back tears while putting parts away on a shelf. There was one gentleman who knew what I was going through, and he was a retired nuclear technician from the navy. His job at the bike shop was more of a hobbyist and enthusiast of motorcycles than anything else. His wife made the money, and he just put the time in.

Life was pretty bleak then because all I had were the bike shop, home, and my computer, and I was looking for a new job. At least I had my KLR650 and my friends, my health, and some fun at the beach. It helped get me through those days knowing that the weekend was coming. Playing volleyball at the beach with the white sand between your toes and the sun and the sky was really awesome. I did notice that as time went on, I spent more time on the bike than I did at the beach and that riding around a lot made me start to gain some weight. This was where my body started to transition, and I didn't notice it, but the road to skinny fat is where you are skinny but there is more fat than muscle.

Every day I would go in there and give it my best. I would look at what it was I was doing whether it was reading parts off manifest and then finding out where they go in the shop and entering it into the computer. I would even talk to customers at the desk to find out what it was that they wanted to know and get the parts catalog that they might need to find and hunt down the parts or find the person that was better educated to pursue their request.

Later that summer, I ended up picking up some work doing it work for a guy whom I met at an electric company looking for someone to configure a Cisco ASA appliance with which I never really had any experience. However, I was a capable person. I did understand code, and I had a little bit of experience with the language and this Cisco PIX firewalls from I believe it was at the casino or somewhere. I drew upon this and was interviewed for the position. They hired me, so I started to work there a couple days a week after hours until eventually I just quit working for the bike shop and then started doing this gig.

Now I was single, and I had a motorcycle, just living and having to pay my rent, gas, and some food. That was pretty much my bills. The truck was paid off. I did recall riding around a lot on that bike stopping over at people's places to pick up lunch or dinner at home or at my brother's house. Eventually, over time, I was able to get the Cisco ASA to within three lines of code, perfect for production firewall rules including NAT (Network Address Translation), all this other stuff. I had a couple of hang-ups on the configuration where I was trying to establish some security before accessing it, and it was an incorrect method. Cisco TAC helped get it working 100 percent. What I should have been doing was establishing access first and then putting in the firewall rules.

Through a lot of praying and looking to God for direction, I was still able to support my missionary friends who were going away to the country where their parents served when they were children. So I ended up making a web page for one of them who went back to serve for a short term. I supported him with my expertise in technology and everything like that to keep people up to date on what he was doing in Brazil, and I think we bonded very well. We also played a lot of volleyball together.

It was through this time that God had spoken to me about looking to Him for direction and counting on Him for providence. It was during the worst of times when I was making so little and not in my profession that I was able to see God work in my life. I was cast out and rejected from one job offer to another offer to fall on my face in a bike shop. I eventually got back on top. Later in the summer, I eventually had a job offer at a pharmaceutical company in the area. What I know now about pharmaceuticals I did not know then, but I know now that I'm glad I do not work there, and I did gain some experience, but I believe why they are in business is not 100 percent to help people. This was back in 2005 to 2007. I worked at the pharmaceutical for two years, and then again, I was let go.

This was where the most alienating feeling one could ever experience occurred to me while at work. I was working one day at my cube, when suddenly behind me were a security guard and an HR person asking me to pick up my things and leave. I was so taken aback by this request that my jaw could not have hit the floor any harder than it did. I felt like a criminal and a suspect and as if I had done something wrong. It was so bad that I held my hands up. I backed away from the computer and touch nothing and walked away with nothing but my clothes like my jacket. They told me to pick up my jacket and follow the guard to my car. I then asked what happened and what I did to deserve that.

I tried looking at my colleagues' faces as I was leaving to look for clues and for anyone to give me an answer to what happened. I was there for a total of two years, so if there was something suspicious about my performance, it would have been evident in six months to a year. Later, I realized it was not my performance; it was my request for more pay. The manager realized I had opened my eyes to what my bill rate was compared to what I was getting. The company was making more money on my head than they were putting into my pocket.

Now I hope you are sitting down, and you were ready for what I'm about to explain next. This fall from grace if you will was so bad because we had just gotten married. We had just purchased a house. This was our first home together outside an apartment. In addition, I had just bought a used truck since we lived in the country and owned a home. What happened here put my wife in a fetal position crying buckets of tears because I was let go. Her faith in me was shaken and broken. I tried to tell her that I believe it was because I requested more compensation based on what I've found out about the bill rate. Nothing seemed to set her at ease. What I did do with my time was clean up around the house we had just purchased.

We purchased the house in November, and then on March 27, 2007, a Wednesday, I lost my job. What would a man do with this news and situation? I had a wife and a new house, and we were trying to build our lives together. This would have been the hair that broke the camel's back. Because not only was she going through separation anxiety issues from her home country but also due to my independent, determined, raw, and impulsive ways. I mentioned to you earlier that while there are big decisions in life that I have figured out, it is the focus on the small things that I need to do. I believe this was what she feared more on top of being unemployed. What's cool was that later after marriage and meeting my wife at a casino, our next jobs were more prestigious as we both worked at the pharmaceutical company. What's funny was that she took the job that I turned down for the recruiting job at the vocational training school. Anyway, she was working, and I was unemployed.

What did I do, you would ask? That's a good question. I eventually went back to the casino. This time I got the position that I wanted. I was a surveillance technician with access to video surveillance and network equipment. It was from here that my IT career took off. In 2008, I ended up getting a Cisco certification, and then I went for another certification in security. My work in the casino was short term. I was able to learn and demonstrate my experience with Cisco networking technology, and that built the foundation for me to get into cybersecurity. I had some personality issues at this place. I had a nemesis, someone who was miserable and challenged me almost physically.

Then there was an altercation. Some discipline was taken against the individual as he was trying to micromanage me, judge me, and be critical of me. What's funny was that he showed a side of himself that was a part of me, but I never knew I sounded like that to any person at home or at work. More of this revelation comes from my wife's perspective. But he represented the dark path of villain would take in a movie. There were days that he would make snide remarks to provoke me, and I went to find opportunities to knock his block off. I fought it back. I prayed and asked God to help me with this situation because I so wanted to punch this individual but that would tarnish my career.

When I left the casino, I went on to work at a school and revise their entire campus network with new equipment in eight weeks. It was my former high school. Are you ready for another challenge? Shortly after working at the school, I left to go work for a company that I coined the name from, something in the Automotive World but applying to the Network World. I was going again for this entrepreneurial spirit that was inside me. It was so hard to keep this self-driven and motivated spirit set aside. Even to this day, I still have the company, and I still have a day job. I used this as a vehicle obviously to win in this race of life as well as a tax tool. It also gives me the autonomous ability to speak freely and not worry about when or where the next check is coming from. That, my friend, is why I say, "Never again," in the voice of Batman. I am so resolute in my way which has become a part of me, and I have, through the grace of God, embodied the essence of the story.

While working at the school, I had some major decisions to make yet again. In addition, I had a near-death experience to tell you about. In the latter half of the first decade from 2000 to 2010, I made the choice to leave the casino once and for all for a more reputable job in a school. At that time, I was becoming a father for the first time. My oldest was born in late fall. Decisions had to be made as I was burdened with her and with in-laws under the same roof. Money was just not plentiful. I still had the private practice, but it was not enough. As always, it took time away from the family, or soon-to-be family.

In the following spring, we had a company outing at the local baseball field. It was a minor league team in which we attended in a skybox room or bleachers right in front of right field. While talking among friends and locals of the area and eating some party food, the baseball game went on. Then came one of the cleanup hitters. He was up at bat and fouled the first ball. I turned my head and continued the conversation. All of a sudden, he connected yet another foul ball, but this one had some heat on it, and it popped right to where I was standing.

There I was gabbing away, and I looked at the people's faces, and people were yelling, "Look out!" Sure enough, it was 80 miles an hour uphill straight to my face. At the last moment I turned to see, and something moved me. I did not have time to move myself. I was going to be a vegetable had I stayed right there. The ball bounced off the back of the skybox and still hit me in the arm, in the triceps area. Days later I had a black, blue, end even green mark.

Ladies and gentlemen, let me tell you, God was in control there. Something from another dimension moved me out of harm's way. I am here today for that so I can write to you. When God has a plan for you, it is written in heaven above. We must look to Him for His leading, so we don't miss out on the blessing. It is always better to give than receive and best of all to give of yourself to help others. I was so amazed that I told this story for weeks. God had a plan and a purpose for me and kept me alive so that I could be here today to write this book or I could talk to someone at the gym. You never know when God is going to use you, but when He's done with you, He will call you home.

Everything was going fine. I was working at a school and had in-laws living with me in a small house with stubborn personalities. Okay, some humor there. Life was going, and then I realized because of the situation and the food bills, a little more money wouldn't hurt. The school wanted me to drop my side business, as some calls came in during the day. I tried, but I just couldn't. I knew I could do better. I was approached by a contractor to work for him doing independent insurance adjusting. It sounded good in the brochure. I was so hesitant though; it should have been a warning. I had unsettling feelings about it when he said, "Sure, you can still work your private practice."

I had a hard time leaving the school that I almost wanted to rescind my resignation letter as I had that gut instinct telling me it was not going to go smoothly, but it was too late. I was marched out from my job to my car as I was a risk. I was not really a risk, but to be on the safe side, they did let me go. Hardest apple to swallow yet again. Now I really needed to make independent adjusting work and the report writing be perfect. The Holy Spirit was working on me, but I didn't listen, and at the same time, it was going to make me stronger.

When the time came to be that independent adjuster, and if I was working for me doing network and computers, then I would not get new claims in to process. It was all downhill. What looked like a great opportunity came into a bunch of excuses. First, he said my reports were written in the wrong tense. It had to be third-person perfect. Later, I found out that expert testimony used the first person and exonerated me from this egotistical "friend's" judgment call. Meanwhile, my wife was freaking out. Yet another job that I was bouncing from as it seemed every two years. This time it was just five months. There were some other peculiar issues going on as well. I used to drive on-site to my friend's house to work across him at a computer, and his wife was always walking by and looking or commenting. Later they ended up moving to Florida. I think other things were going on not on the surface, but there were some clues my friend mentioned that I had no idea. I really don't understand body language unless someone comes right out and tells me they like me or has a crush or they have an office crush.

This was where I wanted to take a moment here to talk to you about all the challenges that I had from 2000 to 2011. If it had not been for my faith in Christ, I would not be able to get on my knees and ask for help from my heavenly Father because something else in life would have taken over. My upbringing, my training, and my experiences in my youth and scripture memorization helped equip me for the challenges that life was going to give me. I praise and thank God for the wonderful mind that He gave me so that I can remember so much information that I can understand and learn and deliver solutions based on the technology that was in place and how it worked. I also want to take this time to show you that while you may not be gifted with a great memory or technical expertise, what you can be is a willing person to let God take over parts of your life. He will take you places that you've never dreamed of.

Faith is the bridge where hope falls short.

Letting go and letting God is not easy. Sometimes we think we know better. *Perhaps I can give God a hand today.* Has that thought ever crossed your mind? When a person first comes to Christ, they are pumped up (a '90s term) to get moving for God. They want to progress down the path that they miss out on earlier in their lives. While some testimonies show people on the brink, others are not so dramatic. What needs to happen is for the newborn believers to continue walking in faith surrounded by Bible-believing and Bible-living Christians.

On the news, you hear that a pastor did this or that, or some person messed up that you wouldn't expect. We are all human and prone to mess up; however, a true Christian seeks forgiveness and repentance and turns 180 degrees from their ways. Not all the years of a Christian are going to be stellar. There will be challenges, successes, failures, and sin. The only way to end it is to not forget what brought you here, the saving grace of Jesus Christ, and His mercy for your soul. Some say we're appointed and reserved before birth and focus way too much on God's sovereignty than our responsibility. While I give that some credit and thought, still, it all comes down to free will and the heart. If your heart is in the right place, and you are consciously trying to live right, then I say brethren, well done. That's from a human, but I think God would agree.

If you however profess one thing and do another, I'd say you better go check that title back in at the library because you're not trying hard enough. All you need is an open mind, a receptive heart, and a willingness to let some things go to God. In time, you will learn to give more over to Him and look for the doors He wants open for you to walk through, than the ones you researched. There is more to this as there are dark parts of human behavior and life such as addictions that need to be worked on, but for this part, we're talking about realizing to decide to change.

Interestingly while at this juncture in my life and writing this book, I ran into my old parts manager at a local box home improvement store. I mentioned the house we're building etc. He was impressed and said, "Did I teach you some good things." I told him, yes, but I've always been good, I think God was testing me. At a low point in my life, I just prayed and waited. I had no choice. I was doing all I could. So it brought a smile to my face. John, the parts manager, could read my mind and knew my burdens.

My career was moving along even with my setbacks. I was able to make a legal company that is my side hustle and make the best of it. Next were a few corporate positions, and that would bring us to here right now with the book in your hand. Day job and night job are jelling, and I am making wins. The business is growing little by little, and I brought on some help. I am attempting to train the next generation as we move along. This will be the last mention of the career and making it happen as things are falling into place. There are still struggles, but the problems are changing and are really opportunities.

Chapter 6

Listening and Experiencing the Hand of God

Now we go back to personal and the walk with Christ. During this whole time, God was a part of all my problems and my blessings. While I may not always have the time for Him first thing in the morning, I would get time at night to pray and during the day to research, read, and pray. Jesus is most interested in our walk and our faith as well as our issues, but He left us the Bible with 30 percent of it being about prophecy. As a child, I have always been in love with the end of days. As I have mentioned in the past when the pastor was preaching something, I could not follow or hold my attention I would take out the book of Revelations as a teenager. I believe that God in His infinite wisdom purposed some of us to live in these days as we are at the end of the grace/church age. My struggles and personality battles (myself included) have equipped me to endure to the end. However, it's not just enduring; it is thriving and being a beacon of Light empowered by the Holy Spirit to remain supercharged in the name of the true and living King of Kings.

Here we are working alongside each other in life, my wife and I, and the kids are growing and getting bigger. One is trying to be a teenager before their time, the other is a bossy, cute girl with Dad wrapped around her finger. What is interesting is that I try to be still long enough to listen to God's leading. I miss the days riding a dirt bike in the woods or peeping leaf, as they call, it in the woods. New Hampshire calls me, especially in the fall.

As of late, we are all witnessing some apocalyptic events happening around the world. Since the Obama years, we are watching a drastic shift toward satanic elements: the splitting of the home, single parents, easier divorce options, and abortion being a thing despite being overturned and back to the state level. Everything goes against what God has said—to go forth and be fruitful and multiply. We can or should when economically, or both parents are ready for this.

Not all of us were ready or made for large families. The trend is for smaller families. I am one of those, but the reason is so I could focus on living in a multicultural home. Kids are great and a blessing from God. Having children teaches us management skills and gives us a microcosm of the world God sees. If we were to draw parallels between our heavenly Father and us being fathers, we can see there is a lot of responsibility and power. We all need to respect that and emulate it. This is not being taught in today's ideology. It's single parents, abortion if it is right for you, and the government helps with the murder.

Now I know people reading this are going to be offended or even hurt because of the decisions you made or were a part of at some moment in your life. There is forgiveness, and He is there for that. You have to understand that the devil wants to let you doubt what you should be doing and your place in the grand scheme of things. All too often, the culture of self-care and indulgence is marketed on Instagram and Facebook. While taking care of your health is one thing, making it a sole objective is another. Also the claims that we are gods ourselves seem to be a subliminal message. The fallen are supernatural but are not God's, and while they have this power, they think you can too. Soon AI and transhumanism will take over.

The world is moving and setting the stage for the beast system, the mark of the beast, one world, religion, and government. Recently we have seen a video where the Pope is working with and signing treaties with other religions to embrace their differences. The Pope owns a telescope in the US called the Lucifer telescope. Some think that of the three-legged stool of non-nation states, UK Buckingham Palace,

Washington DC, and the Vatican, the Vatican will be the one to usher in the alien deception. Have you ever watched the *Prometheus* movie? This is the story where humans travel to the place where the source of earth life began. That we came from aliens. Watch it, and it may happen after the church leaves where I hope you are not left behind. If you have this book, read it, and turn to Christ. Suffer as a martyr, but you will be exonerated.

What I have been seeing as Jesus leading me in my life has put me right here. I am currently at the last house before we leave this planet. There is so much to prophesize that I am going to try and condense everything here, but I do not want to shortchange you. I'm just a tape recorder, a messenger of what I have seen or experienced. I am in no way saying I am a prophet, but I catch a glimpse of messages while asleep after praying for what is coming. Now are you ready for the story of how we got to the place we are in now?

Going back to my wonder years, I used to ride the bus home. Every day on the way home, I would pass a lot of land just two roads from my childhood home. I looked over my right to see the way the light of the western sun would set and pass through the trees on this lot. It was very inviting, but of course, I never trespassed as I was a goody-two-shoe son.

One day I was driving to my parents in the fall of 2013. Driving down the road, I noticed some activity on the right side of the road. People were tossing nipper bottles and trash, which made me so angry to see people trash God's creation. I must walk myself out of my rage. The sellers were in the process of listing it. They had set up all the typical site work silt fencing. I couldn't believe this place was going to be sold. Just like catching a glimpse of something pretty, I had to turn back and take another pass. I get to the four corners and turn right back down the hill. As I cruised on by, I caught one of the owners walking with a site plan in his hand. I asked, "Is this for sale?"

He responded, "Yes, and you can reach out to our listing agent." I couldn't believe it. I was so excited like winning the lottery or coming from your first date. I drove home to tell my wife and of course my parents. I prayed about it for sure but was so moved I was not sure I deliberated long in talks with God.

This place was a jungle, full of bittersweet, life-choking, vine-gripping trees and taking their lives. I spent seven years clearing the place out, and in the year 2020, we were to start building our house in 2020. How do I know we were to build in 2020? One day while I was where the detached garage is now, I looked up to the northwestern sky and saw a light and then a face and then a torso. The sun was a good 20 degrees south of that as it was October at around 5:30 p.m. I didn't write the day down, and I know you're all wishing I did. I saw an angel or the angel of the Lord—no wings, only showing his torso only with his head and face, and I could see a beard. The face looked exactly like the painting Akiane Kramarik did call the Prince of Peace. His right arm was pointing down at the place where the house would be built. He was smiling, almost laughing as his hair was moving. I was going to snap a picture, and a part of me wishes I did as maybe more would believe me. However, I didn't want to lessen or cheapen the vision, and also, it would be whitewashed out anyway since it was light and bright. It was not the sun. It was October, seven years after that we bought the place. I have never seen any leading like that in my life. I never saw this over the other house.

What does this mean? I am wondering too, but this was all after the COVID-19 outbreak. Yes, the PLANdemic instills fear and dependence on the satanic system and not confidence, boldness, and faith in the Lord of Host's system.

Is this where we make the last stand? I often say I am not afraid of dying, the passing will suck, but moving on to the next life will not. I have to say I am not a holy roller or a pastor or anything. I am what you call a passionate person who deeply loves and adores his Savior, but at times I can mentally get the best of myself. That is where all my good and bad start and end. Good starts there and continues outside this. The bad in me starts here and dies here. One thing I have learned over the years that you need to be aware of is that everything, every good and bad thought, starts in the mind. It is most driven by the heart but the mind must converse with the Holy Spirit and confide in Him all our wonders, sorrows, joys, and problems. The way to survive this life and get ready for the next, we must die to ourselves. Pick up His cross and follow Him. Not that we can ever take His place, but we must share in what suffering and walking in His footsteps mean. The gift of salvation is free; the walk afterward is so very hard.

Fall is the most wonderful time of the year for me, and I have a hard time not being outside. I get very angry with my family if I am doing chores inside versus outside. I love the color and the brightness. I love the fresh air and the newness of the morning. Our lives in Christ can be the same thing. Where we die to self, and let go, and let God, He takes over. Cast all your burdens on Him as He stated that He can take it all. Our bland green-colored leaves like everyone else turn to yellow gold, or bright red, maybe maple orange. We then shine and stand out.

I long so much for the Lord's return. You are probably here because you have questions and are frustrated with life, the people around you, or even yourself. You ask yourself, "Why am I here? I'm not here living but why am I here in this situation?" God has a purpose for your life and those around you. You may be an example from which others need to learn, or you may be the one who needs to learn, or both. Life is not fair or kind. Some are blessed, some have horrible experiences, and some appear to be blessed. I can say one thing with assurance of being in the middle. You are God's dream. He knitted you in your mother's womb and knew you before you appeared. His purpose is for you to find faith in Christ, be redeemed for your sinful ways, draw near to Him, live at peace with others, and show His work in your life to others.

It may not be the glamorous life that others have that will be yours, but you can be at peace knowing that you are living the life He wants you to live. Spend time in His word, read, and have fellowship with others. Also get time alone where you can just think and pray. Ask God to guide you in your decisions. He's not just there when the chips are down but when the things are good as well.

I Am God's Dream

He alone sleeps His will.
My life to be greater still.
Fashioned like clay, a potter's hold,
to fit and become His mold.

Since birth, my legacy has already started.
History written from conception now departed.
Out in this world, I am a thought,
That lives forever, His sacrifice bought.

Now it seems a prayer to be
beckoning thought it calls to me.
Answered prayer a life I live,
From the lips of God, a will He gives.

Coming through loud and clear,
God's dream, His will, I hear.

Interesting to say that at the time of this writing, in October 2022, a lot has been going on in the world: the war in Ukraine and Russia, America suffering from the attacks by the devil, and the left tearing down such a great nation, world economic forum and one world agenda, and schools where children now suffer drag shows and identifying as anything other than what they are born with. Are we in the last days? Some think that we are in the last of the end of days, and up to about a few weeks ago, I thought something epic was going to happen on September 26, the first day of the feast of trumpets. I had two dreams back-to-back, and one happened the next day. The other one is yet to happen, but it was the end of the church age. I know it's written that no one knows the day or the hour, but you kind of get the feeling (if you have any morals and inner pulling from the spirit) that something is just way out of line. The world wants to come after your children and your God-given choice to decide what goes in your body.

As the body of Christ gets ready for the bridegroom to come, we are all trying our hardest to live the cleanest. Satan is now attacking us at an all-time high record to try to diminish the work of the Lord. I know I've been delayed a few times. You know that feeling you get, kind of like coincidence or happenstance? I watched to *SkyWatch TV* broadcast in an interview with Jonathan Cahn on September 18. In this video, at 11:36, Jonathan Cahn mentioned the same term that hit me about six weeks ago in church (while my mind was traveling about recent events and the handbasket the world is falling in), the words, "As it gets darker, the lights will get brighter." We are the lights. This was totally on point with the struggle and with what's happening around the world. The clock is ticking, folks and the remnant are connected. Isn't that just an uncanny mention of the same thought?

I believe this is exactly how our glorified bodies will be connected. There will be some thoughts or subjects that connect us all, and we will know when something is happening. Only then it will be good things. The first time something like this happened that I recall now in this sequence going backward was the hurt I felt at night while two friends were praying for the murders in Uvalde, Texas. It happened one evening. I didn't make the Bible study, and I was not a regular there anyway, but I'd speak with these guys from time to time.

I asked my friend "Hey, I had a dream the other night, and you and him (another friend) were in it. You guys were sad, crying. What happened?" Then he told me that night at Bible study, they were praying for the kids that were killed and the families that were hurting. Amazing right? I like to pray myself to sleep in hopes I meet the Lord or an angel or see something wonderful after praying for other people. I hunger and thirst for truth that is so addicting. I could leave my day job and night job to watch and learn to speak and share.

Just to let you know we are trying and we are fighting for you—educating, edifying, and empowering you to see that God is real. Don't look this gift in the mouth. Look inside you. So let it be said, so let it be done. In His name for His purpose in this life and the next. Amen.

I hope this journey of mine has shown you many of God's interventions in the average Joe's life. I'm not famous nor do I care to be. I'm not super rich or poor. I am in between. I'd rather be in between it all and *in the mix* or the fight than have it easy.

This goes for everything in life. If we ever arrive at a perfect spot, we will never learn to reach for Jesus or reach out to each other. This is very personal in one way as I have spent the bulk of my hours working two jobs to get to where I want to be. I have denied my family of my youth some time just to be where I want to be. I hope now that I can rest in my accomplishments that were inspired and prepared by the Lord so I can share, witness, and have fellowship in my last days till He comes. Find rest in this because if your journey is just starting, there will be time, but you must make the time. In the next chapter, I will go over some of the strategies I used to get here. Some are obvious while some need a spotlight to show you how it can be hard to achieve the obvious.

CHAPTER 7

How to Win with Jesus

Winning isn't everything, but in some cases, it's a must because if we don't win with Jesus, we will lose to everything else. The Bible is a great business management book. It tells you how to deal with people, how to manage your money, and how to grow (in many ways). First off is a verse, of course.

> But seek ye first the kingdom of God, and
> his righteousness; and all these things shall be
> added unto you. (Matthew 6:33 KJV)

Does this mean if I always put God first, I will always be rich, healthy, young, glamorous, and successful? No, but it will have gotten your priorities right. If we start to see the world and the kingdom conquest the way God sees it, we'll start to see what is important. This is why some things are harder. A perfect example is a case in point. When you try to do things in your own steam or power without listening to the Lord's leading, you will either fail or get there the long way. It brings us back to a time when I tried dating the wrong people to fill the void. It was not a good idea. Unequally yoked people will always bring you down mentally and spiritually, as if almost Satan-inspired. Don't do that.

> Do not be yoked together with unbelievers.
> For what do righteousness and wickedness have

in common? Or what fellowship can light have
with darkness? (2 Corinthian 6:14)

So I currently am working on delegating (spotlight word) more of my time and responsibilities to others. I work a day and a night job; I confess it does take some time away, and being in IT takes time away staying on top of trends and keeping up with certifications.

So how do I do as I say fully, right? You're reading this and expect a world-renowned answer and demonstrated experience to follow, correct? Well, I have started to hire and train the next generation so I can still maintain and gain in my personal time and business growth targets. Some of us never know when to let go and let God.

You know the addiction mantra at cleanup or drug rehabilitation facilities? You can't, he can, let Him? We need to be doing this in our jobs, careers, and life choices. We need to be silent enough and attentive (reading) to hear what He's saying. So how does this apply to my career? Great question. Follow your passion, but have a backup plan. Meaning work the job you need to until you get ready to fly with your passion. It can be a 90/10 percent split in one year. Then it can move to 80/20 or 100/20 as we still have job one to do. Be sure to take time out for big events and note the successes and failures you have.

I was going to have a table so that you could see it over a timeline. However, it's been twenty-two years since I wanted to just be my own boss and work for my solo, but it hasn't really happened. Your passion and opportunities to work/sell intersect while maintaining a job. It is possible. Today's trends are being the guru and expert of some crises in your life that others may want to learn from. Tony Robbins and his colleague are selling that. However, as I have said, Tony Robbins and Dean are for those who cannot attend church or read their Bible. All the inspiration I have ever needed came from God. Every day I choose Him over me to win over time. I guess they are okay to listen to for business ideas.

This would be the career advice in an abbreviated fashion that I would give you. Do what you love and never work a day in your life. When I do twelve or sixteen hours in an eight-hour day by delegating or swiveling to bend time, that's how I win. We are going to regress each step here in life as this is the career portion for those who have life going well. Your next question is how I handle other struggles like you had growing up, dating, hot moments, drugs, alcohol, etc., right? I got you. We will go there next.

How to overcome life-derailing choices. The simple answer is to follow what Jesus would do. I hope you are laughing. We need to be able to laugh at ourselves and decompress our life and the stress will kill us. Some scriptures that I memorized are as follows:

> Thy word have I hid in mine heart, that I might not sin against thee. (Psalm 119:11)

> I beseech you therefore, brethren, by the mercies of God, that ye present your bodies a living sacrifice, holy, acceptable unto God, which is your reasonable service. And be not conformed to this world: but be ye transformed by the renewing of your mind, that ye may prove what is that good, and acceptable, and perfect, will of God. (Romans 12:1–2)

These verses helped me when things got hot as a teen or a young and lonely adult. Also this verse kind of strikes the Christian right in the brain:

> What? know ye not that your body is the temple of the Holy Ghost, which is in you, which ye have of God, and ye are not your own? For ye are bought with a price: therefore, glorify God in your body, and in your spirit, which are God's. (1 Corinthians 6:19–20)

Jumping here so you can see my view on this. Basically, when I decided to follow Christ when I was four, I turned over this vessel 100 percent to God. Yes, it was not easy, and I honestly struggled/

hated (strong word) sacrificing daily my earthly desires to His desires. Trust me, there are times I am biologically driven to want to fall out of an airplane into a world of sin, which at this point it would be iniquity. Yeah, even I picked up on this the other day. As a youngster, we just overlook that word, and assume it's the same as sin. However, it means disregard for the occasional oops and feet first out of a plane with no parachute right into the flesh and earthly desires. More so now as we near the end of the end of days. See I told you Satan is working overtime. I got some challenges ahead for sure. You know what will keep you and me out of trouble? Scripture memorization and fellowship. Yes, hide God's Word so that no one can steal it. If you remember it and achieve it like education, no one can take that from you. I always say I lead through education and change. You can swap change with challenges as that is what brings about growth.

If you want to change, you must become uncomfortable.

Fellowship is good. Face it, when we are alone and have time, idle hands are after bad things. We need to keep going and growing. Building relationships with people is key to success. It allows that human element and needs for socializing to manifest. What I think is the best strategy is to invest in people and build relationships by adding value. Positive contributions to other people's lives will help them and you get a blessing out of it. We must be careful of those who will take advantage of it. However, we must continue to try. The book of Hebrews mentions to not forget to gather in the name of the Lord. We know that where there are two, that God is there as well. It's a time to share and reflect. Ask questions and look for directions. The process of gathering helps heal and mend the chink in the armor or remove some arrows. Face it, we all need time to heal.

This is so applicable to not only personal decisions but business as well as career. What can I do that is honorable that in time will yield fruits of the spirit, fruit of new converts for the Lord, and better business? Doing the right thing. Period. Day in and day out, the struggle is real. Christians sometimes want to go bonkers walking that line of purity and politeness.

I used to play video games with my brother at lunchtime and after hours before the kids came and when I had them and they got older. I stopped playing, and I grew my business or did more work in one year that surpassed my day job. Be wise with your time. Anything that detracts from growing the business or relationships needs to be eliminated or reduced to minimal time. There is a time and place for everything. Moderation in all things my mother used to say.

Five personal life-choice principles

1. Put God first. Remember God's Word, verses, teachings, etc.
2. No impulsive decisions that affect health long term.
3. Think of the consequences, good or bad, if executed.
4. Does it align with being a Christian, if published or made known?
5. Surround yourself with like-minded people who won't let you fall.

Those are my top five personal life-choice principles of success. Without these, you are doomed to fail or be delayed, or worse destroyed. Mastering the mind and the body takes discipline. If you have people who do not observe these, and they are influencing you to do wrong, then don't hang around them. It is written, if the eye causes you to sin, pluck it out or the hand, etc. This is meant figuratively, but the shock jock statement is to get you to think that what you are engaging in is:

1. waste of time
2. not building anything or anyone up, and
3. keeping you from Jesus.

That alone is enough to stop you. I know sin is fun and sometimes feels good. Just imagine how much you can accomplish when free from sin's pull.

Life changes when you become a believer in the world. The want to do wrong desire goes away, not entirely, but the will to do what is wrong without guilt is gone. You will still be tempted as we are still human. I've asked myself, "If I was a rock, would I sin the same?" The answer is yes and no. While everything starts in the mind, the body carries it out. In a sense, we think of it but could never do it if we were rocks. Christ didn't come into the world to save rocks.

There are arguments out there that people can't be saved, or the prayer of salvation is wrong and not sincere, and there is no way a person can change. However, the people preaching this and predestination are the same people who live in sin. So how does one go from one extreme to the other if they are predetermined and predestined? Take 2 Peter 3:9. It mentioned that the Lord doesn't want any to perish but that all repent and come to him. Yet some people think this only applies to Christians who were chosen at that time.

I just found a great read on this where someone goes through the verse and compares it to God's vision for man. God's grace and mercy are a gift. Free will is a gift from God. We are not robots with predetermined codes and outcomes. I know as I choose daily to be after God's great will and purpose for my life. Although I only had to choose once to commit to Christ, we make decisions every day. I have been doing it since a very young age. It has kept me safe all these years. Proof that while I started off young and right, I never departed from that path.

There are no magic pills or potions. Just like we say in the health industry. You must put the work in. You still must eat the right calories at the right time and do the work. Consistency in the gym but foremost in your spiritual life. Take note of what works and what does not work. I've been doing it there before I was doing it in the gym. I think it's easier to get abs than to walk the life of a Christian. It's easier to be like 99.99 percent of the world. That 0.01 percent, okay I'm being a little dramatic here as I know there are more than 0.01 percent of people who love the Lord. That's why Jesus once said,

> It is easier for a camel to go through the eye
> of a needle, than for a rich man to enter into the
> kingdom of God. (Matthew 19:24)

You get my point. We are bound by this flesh, and we are not rocks.

The battle belongs to the Lord, but we see it being played out in our minds and hearts.

If you find yourself letting go of anything that made you unique or your passions, I hope that you can find the time, a person, and a way to list those and make them a priority again. I know life isn't all roses for all people all the time. That is why it's so important to surround yourself with like-minded people. If you pair yourself with people who are spiritually lower than you are or have behaviors that will take you lower than you want to go, well, you're going to go there. It needs to stop. You need to set boundaries and then move on.

Wendell Calder at World of Life once said,

> Sin will take you further than you want to
> go, keep you longer that you want to stay, and
> cost you more than you want to pay.

Like driving a car, what direction you are looking at is the direction you are going to go. Keep your eyes on the Christian road and follow Christ. His leading examples of attitudes, kindness, and responses are all things we should look to and emulate. Again, the gift is free, but the price is high. The price He paid for our sins and the price our lives will pay to stay with Him.

Think about it this way. Where are you now? I just posted on social media an image from two years ago of me working in the cold of night to get into the last house we are in now. You're where you are now from decisions you made long ago. I can recall the countless times my mother would say, "Whatever comes out of your mouth is the intent of the heart." It makes you want to clean your speech up and focus on positive and better things. It is better to pay a price now in this life than for an eternity elsewhere.

As humans, we are so confined to the limitations of our bodies. We are forced to walk linearly through time. The devil himself is bound by time as God made it so when he fell. There is no greater power than God who operates outside time. He's at the beginning, the middle, and the end. He is eternal and holy. No one knows how long the Ancient of Days was around and bored (if you will) before he decided to create us. Amazingly, an entity so great wishes nothing but fellowship with Him. It was broken by sin. We are descendants of Adam, but we are sons of the devil, the father of lies, as our lives by nature are sinful.

What can break you from these chains of sin, addiction, despair, and missed goals or dreams in life is Jesus. No one can come to the Father except through Jesus. He who has seen the Son has seen the Father. They are three in one. While I have not really suffered through addiction of any type, I have suffered persecution. I have been made fun of while growing up and been taken advantage of in many ways but nothing alarming.

Again, I am the average Joe. However, this average Joe has chosen eternal life and power over sin and death. Christ is in me and keeping me even keel and coolheaded when biologically, I am a hothead and loaded arsenal of pain and destruction. It's all been locked up and set free from my mind. That nuclear power I possess is now in this effort. This book is intended to show you it's possible. This life is a test or a game God has put in motion. Therefore, it has taken me a while to get through to you. I have been undergoing life lessons and witnessing so many things. The youngest of four with a tremendous memory and acuity to see the truth in life.

We are now through much of what I wanted to share. While I am not a licensed clinical social worker or a psychologist, I do know that Jesus can help show in your life your path. If you read and focus on Him and listen intently, you will find it. There are sunshine preachers out there, and there are some who are said to be sunshine, but if they ever listened to the rest of the broadcast, there is the other side. You cannot read media as trustworthy news; you must watch and find out the truth on your own.

The pursuit of life is your purpose. Some people are looking to trip over nuggets or a bombshell revelation to what they are to be. Sometimes we just need to be. Choose every day to serve God, put Him first, and He will open doors when the challenges come. Some may be to test your response or reactions as people are watching. Some may be to bring others closer to Christ for your suffering. While some just may be judgments. It is written that God holds the breath of all things in His hands.

> In his hand is the life of every creature and
> the breath of all mankind. (Job 12:10)

He is larger than the sum of His creations.

ABOUT THE AUTHOR

Michael K Asher lives in the New England area his entire life. He was brought up in a Christian home where love and the fear of God we instituted. He grew up learning and living for God after making a decision for Christ at a very young age. Since then, he was working through the Bible, church, life, and Word of Life Fellowship youth programs that helped cultivate the gift of insightful knowledge and a passion for being more.

Asher worked tirelessly in many roles from fast food, warehouse, retail, and technology to be where he is today. When not thinking deeply about God's game of life and the origins of reality versus what we see around us, he spends his time defending organizations in cybersecurity as well as being a gym and outdoor enthusiast. Surrounded by his loving wife and two daughters, he helps enrich their lives and is the glue that binds the family together. He is a son, husband, father, brother, and youngest of four, a man searching hard to find God's will in his life and to share the path to this discovery.